KJV Romans 12:18, "Not slothful in business; fervent in spirit; serving the Lord."

URBAN FICTION

1: Raised Real

2: Intro to Manhood

3: 0-100

4: It's Always the Chance

5: Red Line

6: Down Bad

7: P.O.L.O

Raised Real

Boom. Click. Boom. Boom. Click was all I heard as the lights in the room turned on and off as though we were in a club. "Yawl need to get yawl a** up!" Pops yelled as he continued to walk down the hall toward the kitchen. "D**n," I said under my breath as I opened my eyes. The clock read, 5:30 AM. I was tired from staying up late last night watching the new videos on BET: "Uncut." Ace and I would put the towel under the door and catch the T.V. on late. I didn't know why the show only came on at 3:00AM but was worth waking up to see Nelly's "TIP DRILL." I wanted to close my eyes for five more minutes, but I knew if Pops came back in, we would have our own version of FIGHT NIGHT this morning.

Being raised in Hartwell, Ga was the most potent way to make a man. The city was one of the most dangerous regions in the United States. It was hard being an honest man in this area. Hundreds of people forced into one place to survive with low paying jobs or no jobs at all.

Pops was a real OG in these streets, and everyone from Atlanta, GA to Anderson, SC would tell me about his life in the 1980s. They used to fill my imagination up with stories of how he drove fancy cars, almost killed someone once, and how Uncle Jeff and he used to flood the city with keys of cocaine. A "key" today is anywhere between $17.5-18K, so I knew they had to be getting them for $11 or 12K around his prime. Just those **NUM63R5** alone let me know he wasn't hurting for anything. He wanted us to do better with our opportunities in life than he did in his younger years. I knew that was why he was so hard on us with his rules and discipline.

"Ace . . . Ace!" I yelled from the bottom bunk of our bed.

"Yeah, Truth!" he replied in a tired voice.

"Are you getting up or what?" I asked, waiting to hear him move.

I had to ask him before I rose because a long time ago, I was getting out of bed, and he did the same and came down on my head. Ace had gotten too heavy for me to go through that again, so checking had become a routine.

Ace was my little big brother; he took his genes from our grandpa. He was 13, but I knew with his beastly genetics and my coaching from an early age, he was going to the pros in basketball or football. He'd gotten his nickname at school, based on one of the characters from the movie, "Paid in Full."

A few months ago, I found out that Ace would often find money that I'd hidden in our closet and use it to flirt with some females at school. And that was the birth of his street name. I liked it and felt it was motivation for him to get more. Pops even liked it and called him 'Ace' at times.

Ace and I were always together; we had a connection that no one understood. I was tough on him, but he knew I was just getting him ready for this crazy world. He was all I had when we started hanging uptown years ago. And even though he was a young guy, he could fight with the best of them.

Hartwell's crime rate was over 8,700 per 100,000 residents. Every year was a 1 in 11 chance that anyone in the city would be a victim. Those odds were a little different for the ones that were in the streets hustling daily. Studies showed we stayed in one of the most dangerous regions in the United States and surveys didn't count hundreds of crimes on people here.

Uptown consisted of four streets that were flooded with activities. Rome St, Savannah St, Slaton Ave, and Reynolds St. Everything a young man needed to know about growing up in the hood was taught on this block. Drugs, females, and trouble-makers were all present uptown. It wasn't the best place, but it was our playground. Ace and I were blessed to have both sides of our family staying on the block, so getting out of the country was easy.

When we were younger, we'd have to get up with Pops and ride to Grandma's house to catch the bus, so we could go to school in the district with our family and friends. I had a car now, but stopping by Grandma's house was still something we did before and after school. One of the biggest reasons we still went over before school was to meet up with my cousin, Siegel.

He was from Macon, Georgia and came to stay in Hartwell after his father received jail time. Siegel's father was one of the biggest dealers in the city and had gotten his third strike after getting caught with an ounce of reefer. The messed up part about it was that he wasn't actually dealing. The ounce of reefer was really his personal stash. I wished he'd been sent to rehab instead of prison, but the three- strikes law had been in full effect. Lawyers promised to get him out, but until then, we were just waiting.

Siegel was my favorite cousin and was more like my brother after a few years together. I looked up to him and admired his bold personality. He was the perfect kid in everyone's eyes. All the teachers and parents were under his aggressive charm, while his alpha male attitude gave the streets hell. It wouldn't surprise me if Siegel walked on stage, and took the microphone from the principal during next week's pep rally. He was that one in a million but just needed money behind him. That's where I came into the picture.

Siegel would drive across town and meet us at Grandma's house. We always knew when he was coming down the street because he would be the only person who played trap music- loud as hell- at seven in the morning. He would pull up full speed then slam on brakes, so the car rocked back and forth. That was how he whipped into Grandma's yard daily.

"Truth! My car is running hot, so you know I'm riding with you to school," he said. "I'm tired of this sh*t, bruh."

Siegel snapped about something every day. He had a clean, brown and cream Cutlass, but the inside looked like his bedroom with clothes, water bottles, and everything else in that car.

"If you clean the mutha-f***a out, you might fix that bih!" I yelled. I was already laughing because I knew he was about to start fussing.

"I don't have time for your sh*t today!" he replied as he leaned up against my car.

He lit - inhaled the blunt deeply and blew it in Ace's face. Siegel already knew bro wasn't smoking, but he made it his business to bother him any way he could.

"Get that sh*t out of my face!" Ace demanded, acting like he was about to tear Siegel into two pieces like Mike Tyson.

We let the blunt burn out and started to get ready for school.

I sprayed down my clothes and the truck with a little cologne; just in case the smell carried into the window. Even though Pops bought the truck for himself, he allowed me to drive. He was barely home, so I drove everywhere we needed to be through the week.

The truck was a 1975 Chevy C10, painted a rust color. It wasn't the cleanest and had a hole in the floorboard. The V8 Motor, Sony CD player, and Flowmasters Exhaust made it a fun whip. When Pops and I used to ride places, I would stare at the pavement through the hole almost the entire ride. I just knew I'd see an animal's dying eyes after Pops hit it if I looked long enough.

I often would ask Pops why he never fixed it. "It ain't bothering anybody," he would reply faithfully. It wasn't until years later; Unc J and I borrowed the truck to haul a fridge. I asked Uncle J why Pops didn't fix it. "That's your Pops' glory hole!" he yelled and laughed as he changed the subject.

"What are yawl doing today?" Ace yelled, as he jumped on the back of the truck. Siegel and I both heard him, but we wanted to answer after we heard our favorite part from T.I.P's "Still Ain't Forgave Myself."

"My daddy send me clothes and always tell me come and see him.

I say aight but still I feeling like my momma need him.
They sending letters home from school, nobody read mines
And plus my Uncles, doin 10 years F.E.D. time.
Then I started rebelling, began crack selling.
The littlest thang on the corner with a Mac 11.
After school I hear my momma holla homework.
I say aight ma, but look I got my own work.
Started interacting with fiends at the age of 13.
Now my momma finding rocks in my socks, glocks in my toy box.
Like damn, why do trouble come to me like this
But on the real, it ain't even have to be like this."

    We yelled the lyrics in one accord like an anthem.

    "You already know we got to get things ready for the "Senior Cookout" this week," I hollered through the sliding window as I looked at Ace in the rear-view mirror, pulling up to the middle school.

  He nodded and jumped out, rushing inside. I pulled off in a hurry to get in the high school's students' parking lot, so we would get to class on time. I didn't have a parking permit because I wasn't about to spend money just on a permit to come to school. I started every morning the same way, trying to find the perfect spot. I used to come late and park in the teachers' lot, but that ended when Mr. Bell spotted me while sitting in his car.

3:00 P.M.

As the bell rang, most students ran out of class like there was a fire drill in process. I wasn't too excited because my next step was to drop off Siegel and then go put in some hours at McDonald's. While it was a blessing to have a job at 17-years-old, I knew this wasn't the life I wanted. I was working my a** off for $5.50 an hour and was only getting 25-30 hours a week. 30 hours times $5.50 per hour equaled $165.00 a week before taxes. Those *NUM63R5* alone didn't add up to success, so I knew I would have to shake something in due time. Today, however, I was supposed to receive a raise; it would be interesting to see my worth.

"Truth, what's wrong with you folk?" Siegel asked, "You driving like a grandma, ni**a!"

I ignored his comments as I pulled into Grandma's yard. We slapped five, and I agreed to holla at him after my shift.

Next, I pulled into the restaurant's parking lot, threw on my shirt and hat, and walked inside.

"You are five minutes late!" Boss yelled. "I will call you in a meeting later- so we can talk about your work ethic."

He was a tall, white man with facial features that reminded me of Rocky Balboa. He was strict and led his employees with an iron fist.

We were cool because I was always professional and helped him anytime he needed me. I knew I wouldn't receive a huge raise, but I felt a dollar would be fair.

I actually enjoyed making my own money and Pops was OK as long as I followed the rules and regulations for working and school. If I handled business at home and kept my grades up, I could keep the job. I started as a kid; washing clothes and dishes for $10 a week allowance, which slowly increased as I got older.

The value of hard work was instilled in me and showed in my performance. I was a hard worker like my dad, but I kept a perfect image like my mom. My uniform was always clean and ironed. I even topped it off with a name belt that read "Truth." These belts were the new trend, so females noticed the swag. I was far from a lame, and it showed. Since I was an intelligent guy with an outer street shell - I was a catch.

I began on fries at the restaurant but quickly worked my way up. I did everything from sweeping the parking lot to cooking the food. The best position, though, was working the drive-thru. The company enjoyed the fact that their cash register was always correct, and I enjoyed the fact that I saw different women on the job. I knew my occupation wasn't the fanciest, so I gained attention through laughter. If a woman came through my window, she was getting game, and I ended most nights with at least one phone number. I was pretty sure that if we did the **NUM63R5**, I'd increased the sales since I'd been there.

This day wasn't a good one, though. As soon as I got into the building, they began making demands. The manager directed me to clean the restrooms, which I didn't have a problem with until I saw it. Someone had come in and put poop all over the toilet, handrails, and wall. The little sponge and bucket I had weren't enough for this job. I found a mop and hit everything from a safe distance. I knew it wasn't too clean, but I couldn't handle it anymore.

"Truth, I'm glad you're still with us. You've been a very valuable employee the last year, and I want to reward you with another 25 cent raise," he announced.

"Thanks, sir!" I replied, looking him in the eyes with a fake smile.

Twenty-five cents per hour times 40 hours equals $10 more a week.

I stood up from the table, took off the shirt and hat, and proceeded to walk out of the building.

"What are you doing?" the boss yelled.

I turned around slowly and shot him a smile. "Boss, my father always tells me either you going to be a worker or a boss, and I've had enough of being a worker. It's time to turn up--- see you at the top!" I yelled as I exited the building.

I drove off, beating the parking lot down with the speakers and pumping the gas to make the flowmeter talk sh*t. I was mad!

I'd been working at that place for over a year and all I was worth in his eyes, was $5.75. I wanted to keep the job while I hustled, so if the police pulled me over, I could have a check stub to show where the money was from. I overheard my father talking to his friends about how that was the way to do things because the police had the right to take any money that wasn't accounted for. I also needed the job to keep my parents from asking questions about my income. Even though I knew keeping it was the right thing to do, I was done with the bullsh*t. I had $1,500 dollars, fifteen grams of reefer, and was still waiting to get my car out of the shop.

It was a 1987 Buick Regal, painted white with blue rallies. I'd bought it out of the junkyard, so it wasn't the best whip; it was just mine. Getting my car back meant that I didn't have to hear pops talking junk about what I was doing in his whip during the day, and I could focus on replacing the money I spent.

I parked at Grandma's house and sat in the yard to think. I finished rolling out my sack as my uncle, Mel, came out of the house and approached the truck.

Uncle Mel was one of my mom's older brothers, he looked like Tupac and carried himself in the same manner. He was always on my a** about never letting anyone disrespect me or letting sh*t slide. Some days, he was too extra, but there was always a time that came along that I needed him and that TTG (trained-to-go) attitude. Uncle Mel and I got close after he was released from jail and stayed at Grandma's house for a while. I loved this man to death and would draw the tool on anyone who disrespected him or anyone else in this family.

"Why you not at work?" he asked.

I lit the blunt then exhaled the smoke out the window.

"Unc, I'm done with that job," I told him.

"I been working my a** off, and the ***NUM63R5*** didn't add up!"

He laughed as he reached for the blunt after a long pause, I knew he was about to feed me some real sh*t. We sat in the truck smoking and talking for almost an hour. He told me that he was proud of the man I was becoming and that I needed to stay straight. We talked about the things he'd witnessed at my age and how I could avoid small mistakes. It seemed like the longer we conversed, the deeper the subjects went. I was digesting the lessons with a humble spirit.

Suddenly, a gold Cutlass pulled in the yard. It was an 80s model with T-tops, sitting on some clean a** 100-spoke rims. The trunk was going ham, while he jammed to an old a** Too Short album. The driver blew the horn and waved to get my uncle's attention.

"Truth, I'll holla at you later!" Unc said, then hopped out of my whip and into the Cutlass. I watched the car skate up the road, clean as hell. "I can't get a whip like that busting my a** at Mickey D's," I said to myself.

Next, Mom pulled into the yard distracting me from my pep talk. She was the type of woman who always looked great. My mom was so beautiful; people always thought that she was my sister. She always dressed like she was going to a celebrity event, even when she was only going to the store or to work. In my eyes, she was the epitome of what a woman was supposed to be. She slowly got out of the car, so I knew she was tired from work. I got out too and walked with her into the house.

"Why you not at work?" she asked. "You better not be missing days, boy!"

I hugged her, then replied, "They took me off the schedule: I guess they're cutting hours again."

I hated to lie, but I needed to buy some time because I didn't feel like hearing a lecture again. Uncle Mel had given me enough advice to last the rest of the week.

"I saw your girlfriend up the road!" she said.

"Mom, I already know you are talking about Nia," I replied as we laughed, walking into the house.

Mom and I kissed Grandma and Grandpa as we entered, then we sat on the couch.

Grandma immediately started fussing about the bills and how someone had left a message for Mom on the answering machine. Mom listened to it and slumped down on the couch. After a few minutes of us talking, I noticed she wasn't saying anything. When I turned to look at her, I saw tears coming down her cheeks.

"What's wrong, Mom?" I yelled. "Are you okay?"

She shook her head, "I'm tired of all this stress over money, and I can't ask anyone for help," she mumbled.

I kissed her on the cheek and held her tight in my arms.

"Mom, you don't have to worry about sh*t as long as I am on this earth," I whispered in her ear as I gave her a few hundred notes from my pocket.

She refused and told me she didn't want to take my McDonald's check.

"Just handle your business and never let anything take your joy," I told her, laughing.

She smiled and hugged me again before I stood up and started to walk out. "If you see John Wallace on the street, tell him I said, "F**k Him,"" Grandpa yelled as I ran past him sitting in his favorite chair.

I hopped in the truck and laid in the seat, while I got myself together. I looked at my phone and saw I had a new voicemail. I listened to the message and heard it was my home-girl, Nia who stayed on Slaton Ave. She said that she'd wanted to talk to me at school, but I was acting anti-social.

She called to check and see if I was coming to her cookout. She'd invited everyone from school and a few of her girlfriends from out of town. She was hoping the guys, and I would pull up.

Nia was popular, so I knew anything she was a part of would be epic. She was an ex-girlfriend whom I remained cool with. Her parents gave her strict rules and curfews, and I wasn't down for all that. I wanted to do more than sit in her yard and talk about bullsh*t all day. Over the years, she became a good friend; as I became a bigger player.

I've always had a way with women because I talked with sense and used my poetry skills which gave me a bigger advantage over these lame ni**as. All a woman around here wanted was a guy with a little money and someone to make them laugh.

And since I was a guy that carried knots of money and had a mouthpiece that could talk a turtle out of its shell, I was that King, and being attractive was just a plus.

Even though my day had been f**ked up so far, I knew that I could see something sexy and maybe sell a few grams during the cookout. I knew that I had been going through a lot of sh*t lately because I went through the whole day not realizing today was Friday.

I pulled out of the yard and started up the road toward the cookout. I fumbled through the CD book, trying to hold the truck in the road. One thing I learned staying in the hood was that you were just average if your "pull-up game" wasn't strong. I stopped at the stop sign near the corner store while I found the perfect CD. I was normally on that gangster music, but when I thought of a cookout full of women, I went a different route with a party vibe.

After I made the left on Reynolds St., I had already seen legs in skirts walking down the sidewalk.

"This is what the hell I'm talking about!" I yelled as I chose the right song and waited for the beat to drop.

"When I'm alone in my room
I sit and stare at the wall
Brother can't find no love at all
I'm going to find you girl someway, somehow
I need you right now!
Search the world, but couldn't find that feeling
Cause your love is a one in a million
Cause I like the way that you (Touch me)
And I like the way you (F**k me)
And you really make it (Worth my while)
I said Woof, Woof, Woof, Woof, (Doggy style)
Cause you're on my mind, on my thoughts
Let me see your body talk."

"Yawl don't know nothing about that Kilo Ali!" I hollered out the window, the music echoing down the block. Everyone on the sidewalk ran toward the whip as I approached the stop sign and then turned onto Slaton Ave.

I was lit, so I jumped out of the truck and started dancing on the girls, who started dancing on one another and around me. Traffic was backed up as we started a small party in the middle of the road. I knew it was making people mad, but hey, I was having fun.

"Aye, Aye! Get yawl a** out the road!" drivers screamed as they blew their horns.

I finally snapped out of it, got in the truck, and continued down Slaton Avenue to the cookout. It was packed and had everyone parking alongside the road. I maneuvered through the traffic and parked in the Freezette parking lot, a store on the corner that sold popsicles, food, and pretty much everything else people wanted. I had to park somewhere that made it easy for me to leave in case I had another play on the reefer or had to leave with something sexy.

I already had sh*t popping before I even pulled up, so I knew this would be a good night for me.

I stayed at the cookout for an hour or two; then I was ready to leave. It was a good time, but I had to ride. I slapped five with all the fellas and gave most of the girls hugs and a little conversation. I was tired from being up all day and smoking with the crew. Plus, I was hurting and walking like a snail. I was almost at the end of the driveway when I noticed a slim young lady bent over in a car. I continued watching as I walked by focusing on how her black lace panties peeked out the top of her red tights. When she got out of the car, she stumbled into me like she'd lost her balance.

"I'm sorry," she apologized as she turned around with a huge smile.

"You all right, babe? I'm just glad I was here to catch ya," I replied, looking her up and down.

She had shoulder length hair and was wearing a cut-off shirt, red tights, and retro Jordan shoes. She was slimmer than I liked, but she was sexy as hell. I knew if I wanted to end the night on a good note, I should go ahead and get her **NUM63R5**.

We stood near the street talking as we watched cars pass by and people still mingling at the cookout. She told me her name was Meka; that she was 21 and that she was from Elberton, Georgia. I also learned that it was her first time down here and that her man had just been locked up in Sunny Brook's apartment. Meka also rambled about some more bullsh*t that I could care less about. She asked me questions about my age, lifestyle, and what was I doing out that night. I told her I was twenty years old and in-between jobs at that moment. Even though I wanted to tell her the truth, she might not have taken the bait if she knew I was a youngster. Soon, I began to tell her how attractive she was and that I would be glad to continue to see her.

"What size shoes do you wear?" she asked suddenly.

"I wear a 10 and a half," I answered.

"Dang boy! I was going to sell you these shoes that I bought for him and can't do anything with now."

I was shocked at the words coming from this girl. Immediately, I knew I'd been dealing with the wrong type of females. Girls my age were always broke and were breaking me.

"Baby, you can keep the shoes just give me your number," I said. "Maybe if you play your cards right, I'll take you out one weekend."

She laughed as she reached for my phone.

"Aye, Aye! Bro, you still got some smoke?" a voice behind me yelled.

I turned around and saw Ace walking up the road with almost 6 people behind him.

"Ol' boy, been looking for some reefer and I told him that you had it," he yelled as he walked closer to us.

I started jogging to meet him halfway, so Meka wouldn't figure out what was going on. Didn't mind Ace bringing me a play, but his timing was messed up that night. He always brought random customers around because, even though I never let him touch the product, I always gave him the money his people had given me. That play made him grind harder when it came to helping me take people, customers.

After we settled up, and I walked back toward Meka. I knew I had f**ked up because she wasn't smiling.

"So you a drug dealer??" she yelled. "I put my number in your phone, but I have to weigh my options with you."

She gave the phone back, rolled her eyes, and walked back into the crowd.

Next morning:

"Truth! Truth! Get up and ride with me!" Pops yelled.

I rolled out the bed trying to find some motivation. I wiped my eyes to focus and read, "8:30 AM" on the clock.

"D**n, Pops!" I muttered as I started getting dressed.

Pops finally told me we were going to the Jockey Lot in Anderson, SC. to pick up more things for the house.

The Jockey Lot was a flea market where several dealers gathered to sell their goods. I enjoyed going to the lot, so waking up this early on a Saturday wasn't too bad.

As we crossed the South Carolina border, Pops began telling me how he'd heard that cops were cracking down in Hartwell and that he wanted to make sure I kept my nose clean.

"Pops, you already know I'm not out here doing dumb stuff. I'm trying to make my money in peace," I replied. "I hear you tho."

"Let's keep it that way," he responded.

As we pulled into the parking lot, I noticed it was packed as usual. I trailed Pops around hundreds of booths while he found everything he needed. When I saw the doughnut stand, I rushed to get in line. The mini-sized treats, topped with powdered sugar, were the best.

While we stood in line, a man came around the corner and stared at Pops. He looked like the rapper, Snoop Dogg, with dreads, and he wore enough jewelry to get everyone's attention. His chain was the thickest I'd ever seen, and it was really shining on his black shirt. His watch was full of diamonds, and like his four rings, it caught the light every time he moved his hand.

"What's up, ugly a** ni**a?" he yelled. "What you doing over this way?" Pops laughed and shook hands with the guy.

"I'm just out here picking up some things, but I'm getting ready to leave now," Pops answered.

After we got our doughnuts, we headed for the parking lot as Pops' friend

followed us to the truck. He helped us put the items in the bed and pulled his keys out his pocket.

"Check me out family!" he said as he hit the button to set off the alarm on a baby blue Mercedes AMG.

I saw that the interior was peanut butter-colored, but I couldn't see the dash because he was parked two rows over from us. It was one of the cleanest cars I'd ever seen in person. He'd put the whip on some offset 20-inch rims. The lips on the rear wheel were deep and looked very aggressive. The tires in the rear were so wide; it made the luxury car look like a hot rod. Whoever this guy was, he was killing the game and flossing hard.

"That ain't shit!" Pops yelled. "Come harder than that next time."

They both laughed, then we got in our vehicles to leave the lot. As we slowly pulled out behind him, I watched how the Mercedes shined when the sunlight hit it. The rims danced as he maneuvered out of the parking lot. I smiled as the rear dropped while he gave it more gas.

Pops and I rode in silence for a while, listening to the music on the radio. 107.3 Jamz played hit after hit that weekend, and while it entertained me for a while, the Mercedes popped in my head again.

"Pops, who was the guy with that clean car? I need me something like that." I exclaimed.

"That was Yayo! I used to network with him back in the day," he answered. "He started working with me at the plant after he came back from New York."

Now, I wasn't the smartest man in the world, but I knew he didn't get that car from working in a plant. Pops could say what he wanted, but those **NUM63R5** didn't add up. I just wished I could get that whip and pull up on shawty from last night. She would probably leave her panties at the house and ride with me in that car.

"Truth, I got to ask you something and I'd rather you not lie to me," Pops said, interrupting my thoughts. "Are you trying to steal dope?"

I looked at him blankly, kind of shocked that he was really asking me about drugs.

"Pops, I got to give it to ya straight. I have been moving a little bit," I told him.

I turned to look out of the window, watching the trees.

"Boy, how many times have I told you to stay away from that sh*t? You really think you can't get you're a** locked up?" he asked, getting louder with every word.

"If you get locked up, boy, I might kill you," he threatened.

I knew Pops would be upset when he found out, and I knew it was just a matter of time before he did. Everyone knows your business when you in a small town.

Introduction to Man

Week Later:

"Boom, Click, Boom, Boom, Click"

"Yawl get up!" Pops hollered, "Truth, you graduate tomorrow! I'm proud of you, son!"

I opened my eyes and stared at the word "MOTIVATION" tagged in pen on the bottom bunk between the wooden brackets that held the bed together. I had written it two years ago when I started job hunting after school. I vowed never to let anything get in the way of my paper, and haven't lived a broke day since. I've been about them **NUM63R5**!

I hadn't been uptown in a few days, because I needed some time to think. Pops and I'd had a tense conversation, and I felt like I'd failed him.

This week had gone by pretty fast, and I figured today should be a good one. I'd gotten my car out of the shop so I would be able to pull up on the Senior Picnic. Today was unofficially known as Senior Skip Day, which was when all the seniors in school skipped class and went to Hartwell Lake. The atmosphere would always be overwhelming for a teenage guy since a bathing suit was nothing but underwear with a different name. Every female that I'd been scoping and didn't get to shoot was like deer in season today.

I came back to reality and made my way out of bed. Ace and I weren't going to school, but Pops didn't know he was about to get Operation: Pump Fake. We would get dressed like we were going to school, but we'd actually go get my car. Ace would drive it back to the house; then we'd go to the car wash. I had to pull up at the cookout with <u>BLACK MAGIC</u> on me. The car had to stay clean; I learned that from my uncle, Mel.

I stood in the closet looking for something light then chose: a Nike T-shirt and basketball shorts and those Red/Black retro 2s out the back.

"Get up, Ace! You already know what's up!" I yelled. He mumbled something and started climbing off the top bunk.

I heard my phone ring and wondered who was calling me that early in the morning. I answered and got blasted out by this ni**a, Siegel.

"Bro, what's wrong with you? You have been acting lame as hell lately!" he hollered. "I'm on your porch, coming in."

I entered the living room as the doorknob started turning. The rattling caught Pops' attention, and he watched from the kitchen. As soon as I reached for the door, Siegel burst in the house, looking like he was upset with the world.

"What's good, Unc?" he shouted as he entered.

"Siegel, I'm proud of you!" Pops told him, "Yall boys are becoming men!"

We nodded, then Siegel motioned for me to step outside. I didn't have a foot on the porch before he blasted me.

"Bruh, you know you supposed to take me to check out the guns this week!" Siegel shouted shoveling me off the last step.

"Bruh, I completely forgot!" I replied trying to sound apologetic.

"You know those guns are probably gone by now!" he continued.

I understood my position and knew that we flowed as a unit. If Siegel or Ace had a business, that meant we all had a business. I knew the code, but I had too much on my plate to worry about then. I didn't have a choice but to take on both tasks.

"I got ya, bro," I promised, "I'll ride to the TOC, and I will check on something for ya."

"Bet." Siegal agreed, "I thought you got lame on me for a second, Truth."

"Truth, why yawl out there bullsh*tin and you know you about to be late for school?" Pops yelled through the bathroom window screen.

I could hear him too clearly to be okay with talking more. Siegel and I looked at each other for a second then I yelled: "Let me get ready, family!"

I ran into the house to finish getting dressed. Ace was already in the living room with his bookbag next to his feet. He was playing the part like a true veteran.

"Lando, we bout to hit the road man!" I told him on the phone as I continued getting dressed.

Lando was my personal plug. We'd grown up together until he moved during our junior year. He currently stayed in Toccoa, Ga, and had really got his weight up after he touched down. The trip to get to him was a 45-minute drive, but the price of the re-up was too good. I really didn't want to bring Ace, but he always went with me on a mission.

The sound of the Flowmaster echoed through the cool and humid morning air. The dew that had collected in the exhaust made it louder as we cruised through the streets. Music filled the car, the tweeters sang highs, and the subwoofers pushed bass so hard that the rearview mirror shook. My palms sweated as I gripped the wheel with a tired hand. I didn't know if it was from the trip or from me, assuming the worst.

By the time we arrived, we were calm and at ease about the transaction. It was the drive back through Lavonia, Ga, that was what we had to get focused on.

Lando met us in his yard, smiling as we pulled into the driveway. Lando was tall, slim, and wore a black jogging suit. He escorted Siegel and me into a grimy- looking house, while Ace sat in the car. We needed his eyes outside to watch for any action.

When we entered, we took a seat on a worn, saggy couch facing a coffee table. It was covered with reefer, cigar papers, loose tobacco, and codeine prescription bottles. Against a wall, there was a small T.V. that sat on top of a broken floor-model T.V.

Lando disappeared down the hallway for a few minutes then came back with an army green duffle bag. The zipper was broken, so the packages of reefer showed as he set it down.

"Yawl said one or two?" Lando asked putting one of the packages on the table.

"We need one," I replied, "unless you are fronting a few."

I looked at him, while he stared into space, counting in his head.
"Aye, bro, just give me $900!" he said looking at the TV.

Siegel and I looked at each other, confused. Tension and silence filled the room as we analyzed the situation. A few days ago, Lando told me the price was $800.00.

"Bro, you told me $800.00!" I reminded him, sitting up straight.

He and I went back and forth a few minutes about the price, and our voices got louder. Next thing I knew, Siegel jumped up and brought a pistol to Lando's head. He started backing up in a panic, slipped out of his sandals, then fell to the floor.

"Ni**a, you see what you've started?" Siegel yelled. "We going to take all this sh*t then, pu**y!"

He then climbed on top of Lando pressing the barrel into his forehead. I was in shock as I stood up watching the two wrestle. I grabbed the package off the table and threw the money in its place. "Lando, you already know how we rock!" I said, "You are my lil bro, so we not going to rob you." I grabbed Siegal by his shoulder and started to break the guys up as Ace got out the car and walked in. He gave a shocked look as I motioned him back to the car. We all got into the car and smashed up the road.

"Ace, make a left on Big A road when you hit the light, bro," I said as we all started to calm down.

Senior Skip Day:

As we arrived at the Hartwell Lake, the pathway was lined with big trucks. Some had lift kits and huge tires. They all pulled trailers and grills that let me know we were in the right place. The traffic moved slowly as they allowed pedestrians to pass. As we moved through the crowd, I noticed a few faces and bodies. Ace tapped me on the shoulder repeatedly to look at all the girls in swimsuits. Ace wasn't even supposed to be here, and he was soaking it up as if it might be his first and last time coming. As we got closer to the back of the area, the trucks turned into Cutlass, Monte Carlos, and Regals. They were sitting on big rims instead of big tires.

As we continued down the road, looking for a parking spot, "I found a perfect song!" Siegel yelled as he increased the volume.

> "Ay yo Dog! I meet b*tches, discrete b*tches, street b*tches, slash, cocoa puff sweet b*tches (What)
>
> Make you wanna eat b*tches, but not me
>
> Y'all ni**as eat off the plate all you want but not D (Uh)
>
> I fuck with these hoes from a distance
>
> The instant they start to catch feelings
>
> I start to stealin' they shit
>
> Then I'm out just like a thief in the night
>
> I sink my teeth in to bite
>
> You thinkin' life, I'm thinkin more like, what's up tonight?"

"You killed them with that one!" I yelled, "DMX rock that sh*t.

Siegel and I slapped five as we parked and posted on the hood of the car. We sat back and just looked around at how nice the scene was. Good music, plenty of females, and the smell of grilled food in the air.

"About three Kims', Latoya, and Tina," Siegel rapped along pointing out Kim and Latoya. The girls walked up, talking junk and rolling their eyes. Kims wore a blue one-piece bathing suit while Latoya had on a red thonged one. Latoya was tall, light-skinned with an athletic build. Kim was short and brown-skinned, with a small waist and thick thighs. Both were captains of the volleyball team and good girls. They wanted tough guys, like the ones in my clique, and loved the thrill that came with the deal.

We joked and laughed with them for a while at the picnic, but lost them shortly after the food was ready.

After the cookout: Rome St.

"Aye, bro. Who is that riding by?" Ace asked, pointing as a car got closer. I looked up and saw a candy apple red-box Chevy riding on some big a** wheels. It shined like new money, so I knew it wasn't from our hood. Whoever owned the car had put it together well: The trunk was going ham with so much bass, and the motor sounded like a beast with the exhaust. The tint was too dark to see inside, so we waited until the car stopped. If it was some out-of-towners on some bullsh*t, today was not the day to play. I think we all had zero tolerance after all we'd been through.

"Hey, is Truth here?" a sexy voice called over the loud pipes as the car pulled into the yard. I got out of the car and walked cautiously toward the vehicle. At the moment, I didn't know who was in that car because the lake was packed and I had talked sh*t to everybody. I didn't know who had taken me serious enough to actually come by, but I was glad she did.

"This Truth! What's up?" I yelled, getting closer to the car.

The door opened, and I saw a pair of red heels stepping out. When I got to the car, I saw it was Meka. She was sexy as hell that night! Her hair was curled, her makeup was on point, and she was killing the game in a red, skin-tight, f**k 'em dress. She was going to make it hard to move on if she kept scoring like this.

I reached out for a hug and held her as tight as I could without being disrespectful. I didn't want to do anything to make her storm off as she did at the Slaton Ave. cookout.

"Hey, boy!" she greeted as I watched the words form from her glossy lips.

"What's up, pretty girl?" I replied smiling at how this girl just pulled up on me. The car was a dream, she was a dream, and I didn't know what to expect that night.

"Hell yeah, Truth! Tell her to call her friends over!" Siegel suggested as I heard his footsteps get closer.

"Damn, she fine! Where you going tonight, sweetheart?" he continued.

Normally, I would stop him, but I wanted to hear her answers.

"I plan on kidnapping your homeboy and holding him hostage for a little bit!" she replied. "Is that okay with you?"

"Hell nah! I'm trying to…" Siegel started as I interrupted tapping his chest. "Bro, chill out. This me for tonight or for as long as she will have me," I said as she smiled and winked.

"Bae, let me get my stuff out the car, and we can go," I told Meka then jogged back to my car. Ace was inside listening to the radio. He glanced at me, smiling from ear to ear, as he lay back in the passenger seat. He turned down the music and looked at me.

"Good job, brother!" he complimented.

"Strap, condom, and reefer; I already know," he said, laughing before I could even answer.

Everybody knew it was borderline to ride with a girl because you couldn't come and go as you pleased. She was in charge of the whole situation, so you had to trust her. The strap was to protect myself in case she put me somewhere I didn't need to be, and the condom too was to protect both of us in case she put me in a place I wanted to be.

I made my way back to her car, where Siegel and Meka talked about whatever. Meka agreed to call her friends over after we returned from the date. As soon as she said that, Siegel began to smile ear to ear and agreed on having a last-minute kickback.

"Siegel, keep them plays coming for me," I told him.

"Like an NFL quarterback, bro. No huddle!" he replied as we pulled out the driveway.

    She turned up the music and smashed on the gas as the exhaust pipes started roaring. I looked around and noticed the custom leather seats, Kenwood dash screen, and the awesome sound system. I knew this wasn't her car, but I was just going to chill and give her time to explain herself. I was excited about riding in this car, but I couldn't act like a groupie as I held back any questions and kept a straight face.

    "So, where are we going tonight?" she asked yelling over the music.

    Most of the action was at least a 30-minute drive, so I started thinking of some nearby places that would be nice. There was a restaurant with good food uptown, and I used to cut the owner's grass. I figured I'd take her there, show my social status, and get her a few drinks so she could forget about her stress for a little while.

    "Let's go to the café' downtown on the square," I suggested as she turned on the main road toward our destination.

She parked, and we walked to the restaurant with me on the outside of the sidewalk. I placed a hand on her waist, let her know I wanted us to be more than friends. I walked closer to the road was a sign of respect that I learned from Pops. He told me that if you're ever walking with a lady, and you let her walk on the outside, that means she's available.

Meka was too cool and too sexy for me to let go, especially the way her perfume smelled and how soft her body felt through the hole in the back of her dress - Shawty was not available at all!

As we entered the café, we were greeted with a warm welcome by the staff. While I spoke to everyone, I made eye contact with the owner, Akoo, who was in the background with his hands in the air. He had the biggest smile on his face like he hadn't seen me in years.

I didn't know Akoo's nationality, but I knew he was from the Middle East. He was average in height, and he always dressed sharply. He was my first mentor outside the hood.

We met at the beginning of my paper chase and hit it off immediately. Akoo had always given me odd jobs throughout the summers. Sometimes, he overpaid me, just to make sure I was straight.

"What's been good, buddy?" he yelled, coming from behind the counter to embrace me.

Akoo was a great mentor and over the years, he had become more like an uncle to me. I was trying to learn everything I needed to know to be an owner like him one day.

"I have been well, Akoo!" I said. "Just trying to stay clean in this dirty world."

"Buddy, whatever you and your lady friend want, it's on me tonight!" he replied grabbing me around my shoulders.

Akoo was really looking out that night! I smiled as the waiter brought us to a table with candles, overlooking the bar near the built-in fish tank. If I had to describe this place, I'd say it was pretty sexy.

As I pointed out the decorations and drapes flowing from the ceiling.

Meka looked around for a bit, then started giggling to herself. "So you are doing it like this, Mr. Truth?" she said as she picked up the menu.

She started telling me about her asking for directions to my house. She told me that the guys in the neighborhood spoke highly of me; she seemed impressed by how my name held weight in this town. She was obviously feeling the way I carried myself. We continued the talk and flirted throughout the night.

"Dinner was amazing," I said pushing the plates of chicken wing bones and fries back.

I had suggested that she order a Long Island Iced tea. I thought she might like the amount of alcohol present in the drink, but I didn't mean she was to drink three of them. Akoo laughed as we strolled from the back of the restaurant like two fat cats. Meka had invited me to her house to watch the movie, "BAD BOYS." I grabbed the keys from her purse as we got closer to the car. She directed me down Reed Creek Highway, and I hit about seven or eight weird roads. As we pulled up to the modern house, I was shocked. This shawty stayed in a million dollar lake house in the cut. It was a real hideaway.

We watched the movie and talked, passing the popcorn back and forth. The conversation was getting very intimate as the movie went on. Eventually, neither of us was watching. Reefer smoke filled the air, and she brought her legs across my lap. Absentmindedly, I rubbed her calf and knee as I listened to her.

"Truth, have you ever wanted to do something in life, but didn't know what people would think of you?" she asked softly, removing her feet. She slowly grazed my nature as she pulled back her legs.

"Lil buddy, really all you gotta do is do you!" I answered. "Don't worry about the rest because players only live once."

She digested every word staring into my eyes. Her eyes were like they were pools I wanted to dive into.

Suddenly, she jumped up and told me to put my hands behind my head. I raised my eyebrows in confusion, but eagerly did what she said. She walked over to the CD player and began to shuffle through the CDs.

"If you move your hands, I'm going to stop, and the game will be over," she yelled as another song began to play. She slowly and seductively danced her way back to me. I felt a cool sensation when she started pulling my clothes off and exposing my once covered skin. The hairs on my body stood up with excitement; I felt fingers, I felt tongue . . . then eventually, I felt drained.

I woke up as the sunlight began peeping through the blinds. My head was swimming, and my thirst was at its max. I sat up in the bed and glanced at Meka who was still in a deep sleep. I couldn't stop smiling, replaying moments of the last night in my head. I was never going to date anyone my age again. I was amazed at how she took control of the situation and threw in tricks only grown women knew about. She actually put the hat on my nature with her mouth.

"F**k these young girls," I said to myself getting out the bed.

I raided the kitchen, then sat on the couch in front of the living room table. It was covered in ashes, alcohol bottles, and food. I grabbed my phone off the floor and saw I had three missed calls, unread text messages, and voicemails. Before I could unlock the phone to use it, a call was coming in from Pops.

"Hello?" I answered, clearing my throat.

"Where the hell you at?" Pops' voice blasted through the phone. "Are you uptown?"

"Yes, sir, I forgot we had something to do this morning," I answered.

"I'm on the way!"

0-100

Next Week:

I walked to the car with my cap and gown on an old iron clothes hanger that I'd gotten out of Grandma's closet, making sure the gown didn't get wrinkled. I had waited years to finally graduate.

My heart raced, and the heels on my dress shoes clapped loudly as I walked down the concrete driveway.

When I got to the car, I opened the back door and folded the gown in half, placing it in the back seat gently.

"Mom said you should take this picture before she goes upside your head!" Ace yelled coming out of the house laughing and holding a camera.

"Hold up, bro! Let me get my glasses," I replied, shuffling through the stuffed car.

The black framed, non-prescription glasses I bought gave me an extra sauce with an intellectual look. I was killing them with the white button-up, black slacks, shoes, and tie. Although my choices were limited due to the gown being black and orange. Ace and I snapped a few pictures; then we saw Siegel's car race down the road and slam on brakes as he pulled in the driveway.

He jumped out of the car wearing the same outfit I had on. He topped it off with dark shades that had square frames. It kind of reminded me of Eazy E, Ice T, or Ray Charles. He was killin em too!

"Boy, you look like one of the Blues Brothers!" I teased. Ace caught on to the joke; he burst out a laugh that fueled a moment of comedy.

"Boy, you look like a nun's brother!" he yelled. "That means you ain't sh*t, just ain't hitting nothing!"

We laughed and continued to take pictures before going into the house to join the family.

Grandma was sitting in the recliner wearing her reading glasses with a blanket covering her legs. She and Mom were watching "In the Heat of the Night." It was one of their favorite shows.

"We about to go get ready to walk this stage!" I announced, reaching for hugs.

"Congratulations, guys! We proud of yawl and really love you both," Mom replied.

"I'm surprised they made it," Grandma responded, then burst into laughter. She laughed so hard that her glasses slid around on her nose.

"I'm sorry yawl!" she yelled as we walked out the door.

"Folk, Grandma's about crazy," Siegel pointed out.

"She got us," I agreed, cranking the car and backing out the driveway.

Minutes later, we whipped into the school parking lot and saw the senior class parked near the rear entrances. When we walked through the door, we were hit with loud talking, laughing, and fussing. Everyone was turnt at the fact that we were really about to graduate.

The graduation director motioned us to go toward the end of the line to find our spots. Siegel and I strolled the hallway, slapping hands and hugging our classmates. It was kind of emotional, seeing the faces that we'd shared many moments with on our journey. I didn't know what I was going to do after graduation, but the goal was to leave Hartwell.

"F**k all this waiting! Let's get it!" Siegel yelled. "I'm ready to get this dip-lo-may!"

I was cracking up at him, while some of the classmates repeated dip-lo-may wondering why Siegel pronounced it that way.

"Truth Toldem?" the principal announced, and I walked up the stairs to the stage. The crowd cheered as I received my diploma and gave the principal a firm handshake. I finally reached my goal and loved it.

"Good job, son," the principal told me. I glanced around the gym and spotted my parents sitting together, cheering for me. I couldn't hear anything they were saying. My vision blurred as my eyes filled with tears; I became overjoyed with the accomplishment.

"I made it!" I yelled. Then I continued to walk to the other side of the stage as I saw my homies in the background. I threw my hands in the air and started stacking, Eastside Crosstown Gangster, and pointed to the squad as I jumped off the stage.

After graduation, everyone hung around taking pictures and talking. I was finishing up another picture when Jason walked up to greet me. Jason had been my boy since elementary and had always been 100 percent real. He was around 6'3 now and had a crazy jump shot that kept him in the spotlight. His parents were black and white, but everyone could tell he spent more time with the black side. He used to always tell me when people would tease him; he would never get trapped in a name people gave him.

"Folk, I'm having a party at my parents' lake house," he whispered. "Make sure you pull up, bro. It's going to be turnt!" He smiled and then disappeared in the crowd.

"Truth, we about to get out of here," Mom told me. "See you at home." I hugged my parents and walked them to the exit. The parking lot was packed with cars and people walking shoulder to shoulder.

I knew what I was about to get into and it wasn't a party or going home. I had to hit the block and chase this **NUM63R5**. Siegel and I both had flat pockets after that last re-up. He looked out for me last night while I was laid up, so I had to return the favor and hit it. Tonight would be crunk because, after graduation, only a few were going straight home. If I knew my peers like I thought I did, my phone would start ringing like crazy within the next hour.

Siegel and I rode back to Grandma's house. He got in his car, while I changed clothes, and I grabbed the stash. Siegel drove off as I slowly walked up Rome Street.

My phone began vibrating and lighting up. I quickly answered.

"What's up?" I yelled into the phone.

"Truth, let me get one," the person replied.

"I'm on Rome St.," I said.

I finally reached my destination and started to rest at the stop sign. The intersection was crowded on the corner of Rome and Reynolds Street. I heard voices in the distance.

"Hey, Truth!" the high pitched voices yelled from a car approaching the stop sign.

"Hey, ladies!" I responded to the car full of girls. As the car got closer, I realized it was Nia and her friends.

"Truth, my girl, Kesha, said she wanted a dime!" Nia hollered.

"Hit a block, and I'll dress it up for ya," I told her.

I was going through the stash to set up and realized Siegel had bagged up most of the reefer in nicks and dimes. It was convenient for the hustle portion, but Pops told me that if the police grabbed me, they would charge me with possession and distribution since it's bagged up.

He told me a story about how the police had him stuck with a few grams, but he beat the case because he said the whole bag was for his personal use. Even though he received a huge fine and probation, he didn't go to jail. I normally just put my scale and reefer in a chip bag on the ground close-by, so I wasn't stuck with it during a raid. Nobody looked twice at trash on the ground, so I could go wherever then come back when I needed. I'm glad Siegel set me up tonight, though, because they were calling for it. Everyone wanted to celebrate tonight, and I was the man with the party favors.

      I walked further down Rome St., toward the projects. Tonight was a beautiful night to grind up this money. The sky was clear, the weather was perfect, and the streets were full of traffic. As my feet beat the pavement and the streetlights guided my path, I began thinking about what my next step in life would be.

      My parents were old school, so their customs were that one was considered grown and independent after graduation. College was a possibility, but I would need a reliable car to drive back and forth. I would also need a job to keep the money going while I attended school and just like everything else around this town, nothing was close enough. I may consider starting school after I have ground some money up and moved out of Hartwell. My family lived in Atlanta and was always trying to get me to come out there. ATL was the land of the hustlers, and I knew I could attend school and work within a 10-mile radius.

"Hello!" I yelled in the phone after the ringing broke my concentration. "Truth, let me get halftime," one of my classmates said.

"I can't do it, bro!" I told him. "I can give you a little less, but no weight this weekend."

I caught another play as Nia, and her friends pulled up beside me.

"I'm glad you on the clock tonight. Doesn't anyone else have sh*t!" Nia yelled when I got closer to the car for the transaction.

"Do you wanna ride with us for a second?" she asked smiling at me.

"Maybe later, pretty girls: I'm kind of busy right now," I answered in a sad tone.

I really wanted to get in the car, but Money over Bitches was the rule in this game. The night stayed steady, and the time went by quickly.

I'd been walking the block for about three hours when I decided to head home and charge my phone.

"Hey! Hey!" a voice yelled as I walked the dark streets. A police cruiser slowly pulled up beside me. The officer was an old white guy with a bald head and clean-shaven face. I'd seen him around the hood a few times: he had a rep for harassing people.

"Son, what's your name?" the officer asked, turning on a bright flashlight.

"Todd Teapedal!" I yelled into the light. I continued walking hoping he would leave. I only had a few small sacks on me. I knew, since they were bagged individually, that if the interaction went left, I would be down bad.

"Is Todd your real name, son, or are u joking?" the officer continued.

"Aye, man, ask me what the f**k you need to get the f**k on!" I yelled, "I'm on my way to my grandma's house to make sure she's okay. "If you ain't talking about nothing leave me the f**k alone!"

I knew my attitude would either make him get out or drive off. We glared at each other for a moment until he said. "You have a good night son. Take care of your grandma."

One Month Later:

The basketball court at the recreation center was popping over the summer. Everyone pulled up whether they came to argue about who could ball or just came to watch. The court didn't have bleachers, so we all posted up on our cars and played music. I'd come a few times throughout the year and knew it would be straight. I sat on the car, smoking and watching the women jog along the road next to the courts. I couldn't tell whether they were actually uncomfortable in their bright spandex outfits or whether they were just showing off their hard work.

"Truth, I gotta holla at ya!" I heard, then turned around to see Siegel.

"Do you know Jess?" he continued.

I remembered our classmate from school. Jess was a dark-haired, white guy, who was pretty much down with the brown. Even though he was a computer nerd, he had the personality of Dennis the Menace. He always found a way to get into trouble.

"I know Jess," I answered. "He pretty cool."

Siegel hopped onto the hood of the car, taking in my scenery. "Jess said he could do fake IDs for $50.00 and a whole new identity for $2,000," he said with a serious face. I could tell by his expression that he was interested in purchasing.

"I can buy beer and liquor," Siegel started.

"Forget all that, bro!" I interrupted. "I made some money last night: streets were doing NUMB3RS!"

Then we started talking about how Siegel felt about the party and what the girls were wearing. Next, we added up the money made and how we'd stay alive throughout the summer. Things were going to get tight with all this static in the streets, so we would have to turn up the hustle. I was feeling the effects of quitting McDonald's already.

We f**ked up the plug and these other ni**as play too much. Ni**as out here will get ya, knowing you know where they stay. A lot of these young bucks lived in the moment and didn't care about consequences. They lacked respect because there were more guns in the streets than positive role models.

I, on the other hand, was raised by some of the elite around here. Pops and my uncles were not going to let me walk those streets without knowing how to move. I learned how the G-code applied to many situations by hanging with the OGs.

"Ace, Ace!" I answered, yelling on the phone since his voice was fading. When I hung up, I immediately received a text reading:

"I'm on Savannah by the funeral home; some ni**as want some smoke."

I was about to leave when Siegel tapped me on my arm.

"Isn't that your girlfriend?" he asked.

My eyes followed his finger across the basketball court. I scanned the area then noticed a group of girls sitting on a black, 1960s Chevy Impala SS convertible. The sun reflected so brightly off the chrome bumper and rallies; it was hard to look at. The car wasn't familiar, so I started looking more closely at the faces.

"Why is shawty following me?" I asked. She was sitting in the back, on the top of the backseat, in the middle. They were all dressed similarly, so you could tell they were good friends.

I continued to stare because they were all attractive with their white tank tops and shredded black shorts. They each had on different shoes, but Meka was killin em. Her black lace-up sandals crawled high up her legs drawing attention to the tattoos on her thighs.

"Damn, boy!" Siegel yelled breaking my concentration. "It ain't a good look to be over her when we got these coming in 5... 4 ... 3 … 2 ...1.

I was shoved in, and I adjusted my vision to focus on Ashley and Liz. Ashley was an attractive white girl from school with blonde hair, a cute face, and a body that could compete with the black girls. Liz was Hispanic, short, and thick. Her black hair flowed down to her waist.

"What's up, Truth?" Ashley asked stepping back after shoving me.

"What's good, pretty girl?" I answered. "I see yawl going hard on the tennis court. Who won?"

"I did!" they responded simultaneously.

I liked them both and enjoyed their bubbly personalities. They both came from rich families and met each other playing softball. Siegel, Ace, and I used tooo watch a few games just to have something to do. We met them at Dairy Queen after one of their games.

"What are yawl doing tonight?" Liz asked.

Siegel looked at me and raised his eyebrows then said. "After we handle this lil business, we'll be free."

As we got ready to hop in the whip to leave, they invited us to their kickback and strongly urged us to pull up. The last one they had was at a house with a pool and had a bar with soda and punch in a glass sunroom overlooking the pool. We were turnt that night, and I made so much extra money hitting those white boy preps over the head. Those 5G quarters were looking fat in the wrapper.

After we left, we hit the block and made a few moves. Everyone was heading out as the street lights came on. My only plans consisted of nothing more than sitting in the yard. I really had been on chill mode this whole week. All I had to do was sit back and answer that phone because no one loved a part-time trapper.

"What are you doing?" read the text that flashed across my phone's screen. I grinned when I saw it was from Meka. And that was how I knew the kid was a mack. I was looking at the phone when it vibrated again and another message: <u>Meet me at the G&T</u>.

I knew Siegel was going to flip out about me switching the plan, but Meka was grown and had her own crib, whereas there was a possibility that Ashley and Liz would push us out the door if something didn't go right.

"Siegel, I'm about to ride with lil buddy!"

He rose up in the seat and started going off. "Ni**a, you're whipped!" he yelled." "Shawty, I saw you with those girls and wanted to test her pull."

Ace burst out laughing, making the situation worse.

"Take Ace with ya," I yelled, "and make sure he does more than laugh over there."

I turned into the G&T parking lot; then she directed me to follow her. She rode alone in the same Impala she was in at the rec. department. Meka drove pretty aggressively to be a woman. The body of the car squatted every time she smashed on the gas after a stop sign. I turned down my radio and listened to the pipes screaming as we raced through the streets. My adrenaline pumped as I followed her at high speeds, watching her hair blow in the wind. Randomly, she looked and smiled in the rearview then kept the chase going. Several minutes later she turned into her driveway, opening both garage doors. We drove in and exited the cars.

We grabbed refreshments and went out to sit by the pool where we talked under the stars, watching the pool light dance on the water. 90s R&B music filled the air as we swung in the hammock. The night faded and time passed while we melted in each other's arms.

The fact that my money was getting low and that the streets were getting hot didn't seem to matter when I was with this girl. She had the looks of a model with the personality of a homie. It felt good to let my guard down and just kick back. These young girls would have been nagging and causing me to spend money on rooms and sh*t. Blowing money was the last thing I wanted to do while chasing NUMB3RS.

"Hello?" I answered the phone.

"Truth, I need you to bring me something to eat from KFC," Grandma's soft voice came through the phone.

"I'm on my way. Do you need anything else?" I asked. She declined and hung up the phone. I didn't feel like getting up, but when Grandma asked for something someone got it for her. My family was strict when it came to respecting our elders, and I planned on passing that down to my kids.

As I turned onto Savannah Street, all I saw were police in the trap. I went around the traffic and ended up on the other side of Reynolds Street. I turned onto Rome Street and into Grandma's yard to meet Siegel. As I hopped out the car, he ran up to me, looking spooked.

"Bro, D.J. just got hit by the FEDs!" he yelled, leaning against the car.

"We straight. I got our stash ducked off," I explained. "The shop closed my way, though!"

I carried Grandma's food into the house and then came back with Ace to greet Siegel. He was still leaning on the car, deep in thought.

"Bro, it's getting too damn hot around here!" Siegel shouted. I could tell he was stressed out, so I grabbed a few grams. I started rolling up as we sat under the shade tree watching the cars go up and down the hill.

I could tell we weren't the only ones tripping about the bust. John Boy rode up and down the road repeatedly. We laughed when he hit the pothole again and made the suspension of his old Cadillac collapse.

"Siegel, call Jess and tell him to make me a new man," I said. He looked at me like he was confused about what I was talking about. I clarified by telling him about the phone I found and the message.

"Call him and tell him Cap sent you," Ace told me. I ran to the car and grabbed Cap's phone. I found the message and responded to the message leaving my number to call back. We'd been dazed in the smoke of several blunts for almost an hour when the phone sounded. The message on the screen flashed,

I will call in 3 days to deliver my car.

I passed the phone, and let the others read the message.

"Let me do it, bro!" Siegel yelled, standing up.

"I got it, bro," I replied. "It's my play!"

I was excited about the text since I would really get to see what Cap had popping.

Things were quiet around the next few days. Traffic was still heavy since school was out, but the hustlers were in the house. Everybody was catching up on movies, trying to keep their faces off the street.

Jess had finally come and delivered my paperwork in a yellow envelope. I began pulling things from the envelope and noticed an old faded family photo. I didn't see anyone that looked familiar until I saw the face of the youngest son. Jess kept the original body but added my head.

"Boy, you crazy!" I told him, handing him a knot of hundred dollar bills. I was ready to get those NUM63R5.

Ring! Ring! Ring! The phone sounded throughout the house. I rolled over on the couch and grabbed the phone off the coffee table. I answered to receive orders and addresses. I quickly grabbed a small envelope and a pen with a pink flower on top. The Hispanic voice disappeared after barking, "5 o'clock, amigo!"

I looked at the time and saw that the clock read 1:35 AM. I rose up from the couch and sat with my head in my hands. I had some pain in my back from lying on Grandma's stiff couch most of the night. I turned on the lamp and saw Ace sleeping on the floor, fully dressed, using a balled up shirt as a pillow. We should have gone home like Siegel, but we didn't want to miss any action.

"Ace, get up and drop me off!" I demanded as I got dressed in the stale clothes from the day before. He slowly stirred and started grunting. "Truth, you crazy?" he finally said.

"It's the money play," I told him, helping him off the floor.

The headlights barely gave us enough light as we drove through the night rain. Ace and I rode quietly, while the music played low in the background.

"Damn, folk!" Ace yelled, spooking me out of my daze. It's taken us 30 minutes to find the car. The headlights exposed a white sprinter van with a body sitting on all black dope boy rims that matched the dark tint. It sat on the side of the road with a South Carolina dealer tag and a "For Sale" sign in the window.

"Bro, if I'm not back by the time you wake up, come to the address." I said, "Bring the fireworks too." Ace nodded then we pounded before I exited the car.

I grabbed the key and started the van. I wanted to check what was inside, but I didn't have time to do all that.

The digital clock read 2:15 on the dash. I clearly headed toward I-85 South so I could get a feel for the van. As I came off the ramp, I pressed the gas. The exhaust got louder as the tires gripped the wet pavement. Since the traffic was shallow, I continued to open that b*tch up.

I was doing well over the speed limit when I noticed: I-75N/ Marietta/ Chattanooga sign. Seeing it reminded me of my older cousin, Dro. He'd lived in Atlanta all his life and had the street smarts to prove it. Dro had carried a pistol faithfully since we were kids, but I didn't understand why, until I got older. Fortunately, he calmed down a lot since his little girl,

Angela, was born. He had a job at a motorcycle shop and had been lying low.

As I drove down Lenox Road, I began to see why Buckhead, Georgia was considered one of the richest areas in the state. The cars parked along the streets, luxury vehicles, and the landscaping were perfect, unlike anything in my hood. The GPS guided me to a small mansion surrounded by an electronic gate and huge trees for privacy.

I buzzed, pressed the button, and when it opened, slowly rolled down the long, curvy driveway. As I got closer to the house, a garage door opened, and two Hispanic guys welcomed me in. My heart raced when I saw the grimy-looking men. I double checked and rubbed to make sure my pocket pistol was still present. I always carried a baby 9mm when I had to do a lot of walking, but I felt I should have switched out the tools last night and brought that .45.

"F**k it," I said to myself, exiting the car, I was immediately surrounded. The men had overgrown beards and wore flannel shirts with dingy, dusty pants. One had his shirt tucked in to expose a chrome handle and a black grip of a BIG a** gun. The other pushed me against the van and took my pistol. It didn't matter because I knew I wouldn't be able to win if I messed this deal up.

They escorted me into the house, yelling foreign words. I took in the hardwood floors and high ceilings. Expensive furniture and golden decorations filled the room that led to a room where a short, Hispanic guy sat at a table full of money.

I started toward him, but one of the guys grabbed my arm, then signaled for me to put my phone on the table near the door. I took it out my pocket and pushed the button for it to light up for one last glance. As I put the phone down, the guy flipped a switch on a little black box that was also on the table. Immediately, my phone displayed "Signal Lost" across the screen. I looked at it again then at the guy, shocked that they had a signal jammer. He smirked, then motioned for me to walk into the room.

The glass table he sat behind held a huge stack of money. The money stood so tall and was so unstable that $100 bills fell to our feet. He stared at me for a few minutes with a blank expression I couldn't read. I didn't know whether I should speak first or just let him set the pace.

"My name is Miguel," he finally announced with a very strong Hispanic accent. "Do you have something for me?"

I didn't catch every word, but understood what he was trying to say. I handed him the envelope and waited quietly as he opened it. He pulled out the paperwork, glanced over it, and then looked at me again.

"Todd Temple," he said, I nodded, fighting every urge to laugh. Jess had given me a f**ked up name.

Next, we talked about his business and family. He told me how he came to Georgia for work back in 1996. He was part of a huge wave of illegal workers who came to the city for the Olympics.

Then, he talked about Mexico and how the crime was so harsh when the cartel was involved.

"Does this money impress you?" he asked, changing the subject as he sat deeper into his seat.

"This money makes me respect your grind, Migo," I answered glancing at the money nonchalantly.

"From this day forward; we only deal with NUM63R5, all NUM63R5 are letters . . ."

"Ace, meet me at the spot in an hour and a half!" I yelled in the phone as I emerged onto I-85 North, I was ready to drop this car off and get my a** home. I cruised down the road gripping the wheel while patting on the Bank of an America-locked envelope.

I felt like I was about to take over this world. I wasn't even a month into my unemployed summer, and I was already holding bands and some work.

Miguel and I had hit it off pretty well for the first meeting. He was intrigued by the way I carried myself at such a young age, and he said most of the young guys who walked into his house seemed more interested in the materials than in the mission. Miguel told me he noticed that when I came in. I got straight to business without a lot of talking, which was a trait he liked.

And since he wanted to see me eat, he threw me a few bags to keep me busy in-between drops. Even though I didn't know anything about cocaine, I knew a lot of O.G.s who did.

Always That Chance

I had already known that crack was big money. If you had a good cook, you could make three times more. It also meant big time behind bars if I got caught with it. I started thinking about what was in the car for me to make as much as I did each trip.

I had been lying low since that last mission: I didn't need to hug the block while things were hot. I put some money in the ground for an emergency. I dropped some money in Ace and Siegel's laps for them to chill, but as soon as they got it, they hit the streets to flip it. I understood their reason but knew it was the wrong season.

In the meantime, Pops and I shared the house while Ace stayed Crosstown for a few weeks. Daily, we watched ESPN and talked about different investments.

"If you want a house, you got to have at least four percent upfront," Pops told me. "And your credit score needs to be at least a 640."

I remembered reading in a book which said that money was like a game. It featured people who studied money and got really good at growing it. Practice makes perfect just like a sport. I used that motivation to keep me calculating **NUM63R5.**

Ring! Ring! Ring! Siegel was on the other line letting me know he needed more work to make enough for his next play.

I was finally ready to go back uptown after a few days of peace and quiet. I noticed how packed Savannah St. was as I hit the block. People paraded up and down the street; cars basically had to stop and let pedestrians walk. The government forgot about this area - there were no sidewalks. The field across from the G&T Sports Bar was filled with bounce houses, games, and grills.

As I waited in the traffic, looking at the kids run around aimlessly, I began thinking of my childhood. Suddenly, my passenger door opened, and someone jumped in. I snapped back to reality and saw it was Nia. She was wearing a baby T-shirt and shredded blue jean shorts. Her hair was pulled back, exposing her beautiful face, and her perfume demanded attention.

"What's up, big head?" she greeted as she closed the car door.

"Everything good," I replied. "You must wanna get kidnapped."

She crossed her legs and then rolled her eyes. When I smashed the gas, the momentum pushed her further back into the seat. We rode around town for a while, talking about our past and future plans.

Nia had gotten accepted into UGA and would be pursuing her nursing degree. I knew Nia had always had a good head on her shoulders: she had all the potential a woman needed to be great.

"I got to handle some business, so hit me later," I told her as I dropped her back off at the Family Fun event. She kissed me on the cheek before slamming my door. I sat for a moment and bit my lip, watching her walk away. Even though we had feelings for each other, she was moving so it wouldn't work.

I cruised down the road a little further then pulled into Grandma's yard. I jumped in the car with Siegel and Ace, who was parked far from the street.

Siegel's car smelled like reefer, and he had spilled all in the console. He had the scale outweighing a few grams.

"Stop giving these boys an eighth and saying they grams!" I yelled, teasing. "You starting to make me look bad!"

However, the music was so loud, neither one of them heard the joke. "What's up, folk?" they hollered when they noticed me.

We kicked it in the yard the rest of the day, just laughing and joking about any and everything. I really didn't know what my future held, but I knew no matter what, my ni**as would always be with me.

As the street lights began coming on, Siegal and Ace wanted to walk the block. I wasn't about walking for no reason, so I passed and went into the house.

Mom lay on the couch, while Grandma sat in her chair with a blanket covering her legs. I sat at the opposite end with Mom and slouched until I was comfortable.

"Mom, I quit McDonald's," I announced as we watched the TV.

"Boy, what?" she yelled, looking over at me.

"Don't worry, Mom. I'm working on the next!" I assured. I expected her to act a fool, but she digested the news calmly.

"Hello?" Grandma said on the phone after it had rung a couple of times. Mom and I turned to her.

"Who is this?" she yelled, sitting up. "You better not touch him!"

Tears rolled from under her glasses, so, I jumped up and grabbed the phone from her.

"When I found your son, he was already dead!" a deep voice yelled.

"Aye, ni**a! Who is this?!" I shouted my anger starting to climb.

"Pac Man!"

"Pac Man, you 'bout to feel something when I find you're a**!" I swore, running to grab my 9mm.

"I ain't running: I'm on the block!" he yelled before hanging up.

Pac Man was a grimy ni**a who walked the block all the time. He always looked bad, like his life had been rough. I didn't know if he was on drugs or drunk, but he f**ked up. What type of ni**a calls another man's mother with street beef? Since I knew he stayed off of Reynold's street, I was about to wait on him to come home.

I rode past the house a few times before finding a spot ducked off from the street lights. It was at a run-down house across the street from Pac Man's house. I parked the car in a certain spot, then stared at the white front door that was exposed by the porch lamp. I covered my dashboard with a shirt and waited patiently in the dark.

I kept dozing off as the music played in the background. A lot of time had passed before I saw the shadow of a man slowly walking down the road. I reached for my keys, quietly jumped out of the car, and crept closer to him. When the streetlight flicked across the person's face, I saw that it was Pac Man. I raised my gun to line up the scope.

Suddenly, the sound of gunshots exploded through the clear night air. I paused for a second, and I realized that I hadn't even pulled my trigger. Then, I witnessed another man sprinting through the bushes.

"What the f**k!" I yelled, running to the car then peeling off. I drove around for a minute, replaying the scene in my head. I went from the shooter to the witness real quick. I couldn't believe someone just blew Pac Man's head off right in front me!

"Aye, Aye!" I heard as I turned down Rome St. A man with dark clothes and a hat pulled down over his face walked in front of the car. My headlights poured over him, and I saw it was Uncle Mel. He hopped in the car and sat quietly as I drove to Grandma's house. When we got there, he slowly walked into the house, while I sat in the car and rolled a blunt so I could get my thoughts together. As the smoke filled the car, more questions filled my head: Why did Pac Man want to kill Unc? Who busted that pistol? Was it Uncle Mel?

The next day, Grandma woke me up early. "Truth, take me to church!" she demanded.

I sluggishly got up and dressed, then drove her there. "Grandma, are you OK?" "Pac Man was tripping last night!"

She glanced at me then slowly shook her head.

"The Lord is going to always keep us, no matter the storm," she said.

I sat in church, feeling through every emotion. The choir had blessed me before the pastor even started preaching. He was a brown-skinned man with a huge beard: his wisdom was apparent by the gray patches in his head.

His voice echoed as he read King James Holy Bible Philippians 4:8. "Finally, brothers and sisters, what is true, whatever is noble," he continued, breaking down the scripture as the service continued, and I gave him my full attention.

After church:

I sat at the table, eating one of Grandma's best meals: Fried chicken, green beans, macaroni and cheese, and dressing. She even had a few salmon patties on a plate on the stove if we wanted a different taste. She was the one who taught me to use eggs to batter the chicken before I fry it. "Men got to learn how to cook, too!" she always said.

I murdered my plate as I thought about certain parts of the service and really analyzed the message. The message I got was that I really needed to clean my life up, and I needed to go to church more because it made me feel so good. The Lord knew my heart and my intentions.

My phone rang and interrupted my thoughts. I wiped my hands then grabbed it, reading: "7-5-20/8-5-12-16."

I jumped up from the table to grab Grandma's address book. I fumbled around the African tribe and cleared whatnots to find the green pen with the pink flower glued on top. It was next to the Bible and candles above the glass peppermint jar. The flower flopped back and forth as I sat down to translate the message which was: "Get Help." Fortunately, I already had Ace and Siegel ready to ride.

While I enjoyed working for the plug, my squad needed the whole pie. So, I was going to hit one big lick then fly straight afterward. I'd been thinking about it for a while, and this plan was coming together like 10 books playing spades.

I created my own message then replied:

1-12-18-5-1-4-25/18-5-1-4-25.

Decoded the message would read, "Already ready."

Redline

Just as I was about to explain the details of the mission, I got another text that read "Come Now." We weren't supposed to meet until the next day, and the second message told me to come alone, or the deal was off. Something wasn't right about this situation I was about to face soon.

"Dro, let me borrow one of the bikes right quick," I requested. "The plug just texted and said to come through for a minute."

He looked at me with a sly, grin on his face. "Hold on, bruh! Why you need it now?"

"Bruh, he thinks I'm making a two hour trip from Hartwell, and I can't wait that long. I need to see what's up!" I explained with a serious look.

He shot one more ball then walked outside. We followed, excited to hear those beasts crank up. Dro opened the barn doors and hopped on the Kawasaki. When he turned the key, the headlights pierced the yard like a demon's eyes.

The bike shuddered then woke up with a fierce growl through that M4 exhaust.

"Hell yeah!" Ace yelled.

Dro walked the bike out of the barn and onto the paved driveway, then revved the motor.

"Aye, let me get the tires ready for ya," Dro told me as he squeezed the front brakes then laid on the throttle.

The rear tire acted a fool, causing the bike to jump and slide from side to side. He held the bike steady, and the smoke from the tires filled our noses with a burnt rubber smell. Fire shot from the exhaust as Dro shot down the driveway recklessly.

We stood in the yard listening to the bike's screams as he pushed it to the limits. He went further away from the house, and the noise faded into the distance. I was ready to go, and this ni**a is joyriding. There were a time and place for everything, and I really couldn't talk sh*t since I was the one trying to borrow one of his toys. I couldn't do anything, but stay calm and let that man enjoy himself.

My phone rang and vibrated, and I saw an incoming call.

"Hello?" I answered the phone, frustrated.

"What's wrong with you, babe?" a voice came through the phone sounding so sweet and innocent. I calmed down when I remembered my Shawty didn't have anything to do with my stress.

"What's up, pretty girl?" I replied. "I'm busy right now, but I'll be pulling up later tonight."

"Ni**a, where you been and why you always busy?" she yelled.

Dro comes back revving loudly. Since I couldn't hear anything she was saying, I just hung up then jumped on the bike.

The power of the bike was crazy, and my adrenaline was at its full cap. As I got closer to the house, I began cruising. I didn't want to make too much noise in the quiet neighborhood so late at night. Darkness covered everything except the small areas the bike's high beams lit up. I pulled up to the entrance gate and sat for a few minutes to catch my breath. The night was quiet so, during the long pause, I heard nothing but dozens of crickets chirping in the distance. It was peaceful and relaxed me for a moment.

A couple minutes later, I pushed the call button.

"Hello?" a voice sang through the intercom.

"Tell Miguel I'm here!" I yelled into the speaker.

Suddenly, as I waited for a reply, a car came out of nowhere then slammed on brakes, inches from me. The lights lit up the area and blinded me for a second. The first thing that came to my mind was that someone was trying to kill me. So, I jumped off the bike and sprinted to the nearest tree. As I ran, I grabbed my pistol and let off two shots toward the light.

"Todd!! Todd!!" I heard in the distance from the intercom.

I lay in the dark, under the tree, looking for any movement from the car. Two guys got out and checked the car for damages. It started running for a few minutes then the gate opened. I kept watching trying to catch my breath. I was getting more and more upset as I thought about how this night was going.

"F**k!" I muttered feeling ants or some kind of insect biting my arms.

Grandpa used to always tell me that "Men show their true colors when that pressure is on 'em!" I was ready for the war if it got to that point. I believed I'd just messed up my whole mission. Even though I didn't like it, I wasn't about any bulls*t today.

I noticed the car going down the driveway and stood up to dust off my body and clothes. Then, I cautiously walked back to the bike.

"Todd, Todd!" the voice yelled again through the intercom.

"What's up, bruh?" I asked, throwing my leg over the bike getting ready to turn around and head back to Dro's house until I heard, "I'm so sorry! Please come in!"

I pushed in the clutch and fired the bike up. Next, pulled the throttle every now and again to hear the bark through the exhaust. I looked down the driveway and onto the street. I knew if I left, I was getting no money nor work. So, I kicked it in first then headed down the driveway. I could barely steer, as I drove using my right hand, and held the gun with the handlebar using my left hand.

As I approached the house, the two men walked closer to the bike. It was the same two men that were always at the house. If I knew it was my boys, I would have never sent those shots. They immediately pulled me off the bike and grabbed me.

As I opened the doors, they slowly revealed the biggest pool I had ever seen. The pool was bigger than the one at the Hart County YMCA. I used to ride by there and holla at my boys on Tater Hill. I knew I could always get a laugh off those guys and make some major moves if I needed to.

"Todd, I'm glad to see you, my friend!" Miguel yelled from the middle of the pool. I walked closer to the edge and watched the lights dance on the water. The light patterns were broken up by a wave as Miguel slapped the water. "Get in the pool, Migo!" he yelled, waving me to come closer with both hands. "Migo, I didn't come out here for all of that, bro!" I yelled cutting the games short. I didn't come all the way out here just to play around in someone else's crib; I was focused on trying to build my own. #RNS

"Ha! Ha! Ha!!!" he yelled as he burst into an unexplained laugh. I focused on him and gave him a weird look. "Migo, get in the water!" he yelled, "You either get in or get thrown in!" I took a step back as I digested the message. I looked at his two bodyguards, and they both stepped forward simultaneously. "Migo, this sh*t better be worth it, bro!" I yelled. "You slick got me f**k up!" I found a chair close, sat down, and began taking my shoes off.

I slowly got in the pool after being resistant. Everyone knew black people couldn't swim, but he didn't care. We were both examples of African American and Mexican stereotypes.

I stared at Miguel in the pool smiling ear to ear. To my surprise, the water was warm and soothing. I swam slowly to the middle of the pool to meet Miguel. "Migo, what you do with my money?" he said strongly as he kept a serious face. The depth of the pool was just above my head; I could barely graze the pool floor with my feet. I focused on just keeping my head above water as we began the conversation. "Migo, what are you talking about, man?" I asked spitting water that was getting into my mouth.

Miguel and I talked about the issues he had on his heart. The delivery truck was hit. The truck was said to have over two million dollars on it. He asked me repeated questions before he was sure that I had nothing to do with the robbery.

"I want to believe you shot at my men because you were scared!" he said. "I also believe if you did it you wouldn't come." There was a long pause before anything happened. He quickly started to swim out the pool. "Follow me, Migo!" he yelled over his shoulder.

I was ready to get out the pool. I was about to drown but wanted to stay alive long enough to check on this money. I swam to the opposite end of the pool, grabbed my clothes, and started to get dressed.

I moved slowly as I thought about the situation. I came to an angry Mexican's house, shot at his men, knowing Mexicans barely f**k with black people, and I'm still alive. I could have tried to leave or never come at all, but sometimes the thoughts of what-if hurt more than the outcome of a situation. Miguel was the one who put me on the next level, so I felt I had to stay loyal no matter the cost in his eyes. I was mad about how someone got him before we did!

As I tried my shoes, I looked across the pool, and the three men were waving. They talked among one another as I headed for their direction. They stood and watched as I got closer. My shoes squeaked as I pushed off each step. The distance was so long and the squeaks had become annoying as I reached the men.

    I followed Miguel into the other room as he preached about loyalty. We entered into another room that was filled with lockers and storage bins. We all stood at the table as Miguel went through the room opening bins and collecting items. He emptied his arms onto the table.

    The pile had a few guns that immediately gained my attention. The bodyguard both stepped closer to me as they watched me gaze over the items. I didn't have a desire to harm anyone but was focused on my defense.

    "Truth, today you will be given the option to become one of us. You do as you are told, and you will never see another broke day in your life," Miguel said as he opened up a few bags he had on the table. I watched as he pulled stacks of money out of the bags, and started to layout pictures.

    I scanned over the pictures and immediately noticed it was my Pops' homie from South Carolina. I tried my best to keep a straight face and aimlessly look over the photos. I knew if Miguel found out that I knew him, we would be back at square one with the assumptions.

    "I never thought you would be crazy enough to fire at my men at my home," he continued. "I wanna use that lion in you for good." He pushed one of the photos closer to me and flipped it over to show an address. Miguel's finger hovered over the address and then slammed on the table. "Go here and kill this migo!" he yelled as I stared at me. I acknowledged his seriousness and nodded my head. He pushed the cash over to me and threw me one of the bags.

I looked around the room to make sure we were all in agreement. Miguel was about to pay me all this cash for a hit. I knew I might be shooting someone soon, but this whole situation went left on me. "Grab one of those throwaway guns and get out my house," he yelled. "Once you take that money out this house, the deal is done. Don't make us kill you that way." They all laughed as I exited the house and slowly drove down the driveway.

I got back to Dro's house to tell the team the plan and let them know we were about to be rich. We got half of the money to do the hit and would get the other half afterward. I gave Dro money to buy the borrowed motorcycles and some to thank him for the attempt to risk it all.

Siegel and I lit the streets up shooting down I-85N like bullets out a barrel. I realized we were pushing when I started to see fire shoot from Siegel's pipe. We turned a 2-hour ride into close to 45 minutes doing speeds over 180mph. This adrenaline rush was better than sex.

I had to push down the highway fast as I could because my body was starting to cramp. My body started to itch from all the road grim hitting me at high speeds. As soon as we pulled into the yard; I ran into the house to shower and get fresh for the night. I never spent all my money on clothes, but always popped tags on some new sh*t. We were just living the lifestyle of some young rich nigga.

"Boom! Boom! Boom!" on the last strike the door flew opened. I was trapped in the worst position ever. I didn't ride down that highway with over $100k in cash just to get robbed at home. "You got fucked up!" I yelled. I pulled back the shower curtain and noticed the shape of a woman through the fog from the steam. "You must think I'm stupid" the woman yelled as I was shoveled through the curtain. I fell in the tub and smacked my head. As I tried to free myself from the shower curtain, I saw Meka walk over me.

"Shawty, what the hell wrong with you?" I yelled. "How the hell did you get in my house?" She folded her arms and started rolling her neck with every word. "You worried about the wrong thing!" she yelled. "Where that b*tch at?" I lay in the tub and just stared at the ceiling. My life was moving too fast for me. The shower pissed water on me while the blood from my head formed tears. My chest was still beating hard from the thought of the intruder being the police, but I was forced to fight insecure women's problems. "You going to say something or just sit there and look stupid!" she yelled as he grabbed my phones and ran out the door.

"F**k!" I yelled as I lay helplessly in the tub. Ace heard the noise and ran into the bathroom. "Bruh, what the f**k you doing?" he yelled as he burst into laughter. I fell with the curtain wrapped around me, so I couldn't even get a hand free to lift myself up. "Bro, she rolled your a** like a blunt!"

Ace helped me out the shower, and I hit the ground running. I couldn't let Meka mess up my business just because she thinks I'm cheating. I ran through the house and grabbed some shorts and shoes. I threw on the items and headed out the door. I jumped on the bike and hit the streets in hope to catch her. The wind beat on my body badly as I increased my speed and continued to kick through gears. I was riding like a champ with no protection. I didn't have on a shirt, boxers, nor socks riding through the streets.

As I approached her house, I saw her car parked in the garage. She usually closed it, but I guess she knew I would be close behind. I sat at the end of the driveway and took a second to gather my thoughts. I'd always believed in the transfer of emotion theory: If I went into the house with an attitude, I knew that would only add fuel to her fire.

Mom's voice echoed in my head:

"Women just want to know you care."

I slowly rolled down the driveway and into the garage. My heart began racing as I put the bike on its kickstand. I slowly made my way to the door, until I realized music was playing in the backyard. So, I exited the garage and walked around back. I spotted her sitting by the pool changing radio stations. As I got closer, she turned around, exposing her beautiful face. She quickly turned away and put her heads, crying, into her hands.

The thought of hurting someone who truly loved me made me sick to my stomach. I walked in front of her, and knelt, trying to wrap my arms around her. Immediately, she began to reject my every advancement. As I threw my arms around her to embrace, she flipped me in the pool. A cold shock rushed through my body as I splashed around aimlessly. After a few seconds; I gained a level head and swam to the edge. Anger filled my heart as I aggressively grabbed her legs. I scanned over her smooth, soft legs, over the abs surrounding a naval, over the smile she hid behind her hand as she found the humor in the incident.

As her tear-filled eyes stared at me, I began to pull her head down as I kissed her deeply. She fought back for a second, but love conquers all. As my tongue repeatedly passed her lips; she began to clutch my back and softly started sucking it each time I pulled it out. The sucking and slurping excited us and began to heat up the moment. I climbed onto the edge of the pool and fell between her legs. Immediately, my animal instinct began to transform as I bit into her neck like a vicious vampire. Leaving her neck and licking down her stomach was creating chills on her skin. As her body began to go weak as she melted around her wounds. As the saliva ran down her abs, I slurped the puddle collecting in her navel. "Oh, sh*t boy!" Meka yelled as her legs landed on my shoulders. I took another vicious bite into her thick, smooth thighs as I snatched her shorts from her waist.

"Aye, who bike out front?" a deep voice echoed from the house. "What in the world?" Meka said under her breathe. As we began to get off the ground, another outburst was heard. "Aye, you lil mutha-f**ker!" the voice echoed. The man ran closer and snatched Meka away from me. I jumped back alarmed at these movements. As I looked them up and down, I realized the wing-tipped dress shoe and creased dress pants. He looked like a square (uncool person) selling insurance except for the pistol tucked in his pants. His face was too familiar to look away as I continued to back away while he shouted demands.

I kept staring at him, trying to remember his face. No name came to mind, and I turned around and ran toward the motorcycle. I kicked and hit the throttle, driving full speed down the road. My heart raced, and I kicked the gears and hit the throttle repeatedly. I lay on the tank behind the windshield as the wind beat my body around. Seconds, after seconds, I began to slowly get deeper into tunnel vision. As I lay down to one of the tight corners, I heard the blaring sound of sirens, and looking through my rear-view mirror, I saw some flashing, blue lights.

Down Bad

"Truth!" a deep voice yelled. It echoed through the concrete-walled cells of Hart County Jail. I rose up at attention to see what the commotion was about.

"I'm here. What's up?" I replied. And the officer walked closer to the cell's bars. I remained lying on the bunk, staring at the wall that was covered with years of graffiti. It was crazy that we stayed in a small town with such an aggressive judicial system, that I knew most of the people. As I scanned the wall, I found several tags from people I'd brushed shoulders with when I stayed on Rome St. I grinned at seeing some names of my classmates. This bunk had held good, stand-up guys at one point in time.

"Truth, your dad said he was not getting you out!" he yelled, "So, get comfortable in there!"

The news felt like a punch in the gut, and I lost any hope I had of getting out today. The impact of the words made my shoulder jump, but I remained, facing the wall. I knew he'd seen that his words added to the dread I felt being in this place because there was a moment of silence before I heard his dress shoes on the concrete floor. I listened to him walk away, then flinched from the loud bang of the door slamming.

I honestly didn't know what day it was or how many days I'd been locked up. I just knew that I'd slept the first two days away, and I still lay on a worn bunk with a dented mattress that constantly dug into my sides. The air was filled with a strong scent of body odors and urine that gave me a pounding headache. And because I didn't have a white T-shirt, the orange coveralls hung loosely: the cold air was uncomfortable on my partially exposed body. I wouldn't wish it on my worst enemy. I'm sitting in a cage, shaking like a neglected pet. #RNS

"Aye, Youngblood!" a voice called, interrupting my train of thought.

I opened my eyes, then rolled over, looking at the elderly black man. He didn't have any hair on the top of his head, and the rest was gray. He was the first person I'd met the day they brought me to jail. In the little time I interacted with him, he spoke wisely and always kept a book in his hand. He said he was in for something about a DUI, but other charges appeared. He was pretty cool, though, because he reminded me of my grandpa.

"What's up, Ol School?" I responded. I was anxious to hear what he had to say today.

"Hey! I heard they have Philly Cheesesteaks and fries today!" he began. "Do you want yours, lil ni**a?"

It took a moment for me to register his message through his raspy voice and broken flow. When I got it, I laughed so hard that I had to take a few seconds to catch my breath.

"Ol' School, if you don't get your a** out of my face!" I yelled. The two crazy white guys laughed as he gave me the finger and walked away. We joked a lot to keep our time in there from being so difficult.

I walked to the speaker mounted under the old camera used to monitor the cells.

"Guard, guard! Let me get a phone call!" I hollered.
"I'll be there in a minute," a voice replied.
"Doc, you said that about two hours ago," I countered.
I turned to walk back to my bunk, and I noticed Ol' School waving to get my attention. I moved toward him and noticed he was holding a worn pocket-sized notebook. The red cover was wrinkled and ripped in half, exposing damaged pages. When I was next to him, he opened the book and seated it on his homemade stand. The entire sheet was full of **NUM63R5** and letters.

"Ol' School, what you got going on here?" I asked. "You got a gambling ring going on or something?"

He looked at me like I was crazy, then signaled for me to shut up because the white guys could hear me.

"Have you heard of the stock market and compound interest?" he asked.

I nodded, then waited for the next question. "Young Blood, these fools out here sellin' dope, chasin' prison," he spouted and began a passionate conversation.

He went into a spiel about how the stock market could make sure you had a million dollars using the right NUM63R5. He told me that 401(k)s, IRAs, Roths, Mutual Funds, and Exchange-Traded Funds were just a few accounts that people used to gain wealth over the years. Then, he let me know that the key to wealth was to have an account driven by the stock market since it could gain an average of six to eight percent per year. And that's why most companies gave their employees yearly cost-of-living raises every year of 3% to keep up with inflation.

"We were raised in a time when our parents didn't have access to better education. Majority of our families didn't have money to invest, and the ones that did have money only knew of savings and checking. I grew up putting all of my wealth into my checking and saving accounts," Ol' School explained.

"That's what you're are supposed to do stupid!" one of the white guys interjected, causing some people to burst out in laughter.

"That's why your ignorant a** doesn't know sh*t!" Ol' School yelled out of the cell.

"Shut the hell up!" the guard ordered.

I came from a traditional family, strong with morals; showing your elders some respect was always a must. My father used to tell me that I wouldn't be anything if my elders hadn't paved the way. Hearing those white kids disrespect my guy was unacceptable, and the anger I felt was like a flame getting a burst of oxygen. When it reached its max point, I walked out of the cell to them.

"Which one of ya'll ni**as poppin?" I shouted, as I got closer.

The guys seemed lost, both sitting there, looking crazy with their wild hair and weird faces.

"I have been sitting here too long listening to yall talk sh*t day in and day out!" I continued. My adrenaline pumped faster, and my calm quickly dissipated. I flinched repeatedly during the conversation, dodging a clean punch. Each gesture sent the guys crawling over one another trying to protect themselves. "If I hear one more person talk to Ol' School crazy, that person better be ready to shoot the one fight," I finished, then walked back to my cell. The entire room got quiet as everyone waited to see if there would be another outburst.

The Next Day:

"Love and happiness! Loooooooovvvvveeeeee!" Ol' School's voice echoed through the cells.

When I opened my eyes, I focused on the "M.O.B" scratched into the wall. It resembled a note floating on the river, and it stood out over the miscellaneous writing. "Money Over B***hes" was the motto in those streets.

The hard pillow rustled in my ear as I moved around, and the thin, itchy blanket was useless. I stared at my feet, and it was like they were staring back at me, sending signals of extreme cold through my nerve endings. The chill in the air caused tight goose bumps all over my body. When I tried folding the small wool blanket under my feet to stretch it, it seemingly lengthened a few inches, but as soon as I moved, it bounced back like a huge gray rubber band.

It suddenly hit me that I'd just woken up in jail another day! I dreaded having to touch the cold, concrete floor while trying to use the restroom. I slid my feet into my orange sandals at the foot of the bed, then started my day.

"Breakfast is up!" the officer yelled, entering the cage.

Cheers and roars let out all at once: I knew some of those guys were starving. Although I hadn't been in jail long, I figured out the recipe for survival: When they served the food, one must eat slowly and save a snack for later. Since they only served three times a day, that snack could save you, or you it could be a bribe.

I'd also been in jail long enough for the officers to let me go on work detail. And just like clockwork, Mr. Walker's old a** wobbled through the door with his clipboard.

"Mr. Walker, why you coming in here bothering us?" I asked, and he looked up at me.

His face was much wrinkled, and his eyes seemed to be sunken in his head. His pale hands trembled as he focused on holding the pen and clipboard.

"Because I ain't doing that d**n sh*t myself," he retorted with his raspy voice, causing laughter throughout the room you.

Mr. Walker was one of the coolest officers to work with. I didn't know if it was his personality or just him not caring about the job anymore. Either way, we were glad to have him around. He let you stay out of the cells longer and smoke on his days of work detail. It was the most embarrassing sh*t to be seen mowing grass along the highway, but after a while, you could urge for the time.

Ol' School and I talked while we pretended to trim trees overgrown into the shoulder of the road:

We were taught that putting money in a bank was the right thing to do. In the world today, the checks from employers are direct deposit.

The average bank owned account only provides 0.01-0.15% interest rate, which is nothing compared to the bank's cut.

The minimum deposits on mutual funds and stocks are $2.5k, but that account should average an interest of +/_ $200/year.

If you can repeat this process 11 more times, you will be receiving an average of $200+/month.

Over time, you will start seeing that your normal monthly contributions are getting cut because of the interest in paying for itself. This process is called "Compound Interest."

"Are you following me, Youngblood?" he asked. I nodded my head once again. Anytime someone talked about money, I was all ears to the information. The most important thing about the conversation was that we were talking about legal money.

Rules to Wealth:

1. Grab money ($500-$1000) - Money set aside for emergencies while you are cash flowing your account.

2. Get Out of Debt - Cash Flow your entire income and pay off the bills, using your grab money to protect you from broken budgets.

3. 6-month emergency fund (Savings) - This should be a separate account that is in a short-term CD or Money Market. This is the amount of income you would need to live your normal life.

4. 20/30/50 (Income) - 20% Retirement 30% Investment/Business %50 Living expenses.

5. Rule of 72 (Investment) - this is used to determine how long it will take to double your money. And it is interest of the investment vehicle divided by 72.

6. 20/4/10 (Auto) - buying cars 20% down for 4 years or less. 10% of income.

First Phone Call:

"Ace, what's good, bro?" I yelled in the phone as soon as he answered. He took a long time to answer, so I could tell that something wasn't right. Several seconds later he jumped into some story.

"Bro, I don't know whom you were rocking with up there in the city, but you got some people looking for you. They describe you, and aske for Todd!"

The news almost made me drop the phone, and I slowly wiped my face, and tightened my lips, fighting the urge to yell. The concrete wall would cause an echo through the building, and I knew any kind of disturbance would cut this call short.

We continued talking so I could get to my reason for calling. I had to shake something quick!

"Ace, listen to me carefully," I spoke in a stern tone so he could focus and understand how serious I was.

"Shoot," he replied.

I knew I had to hit him with something that was direct, but not too obvious. I tapped myself on the forehead, trying to think of something.

"Go-kart track, red house, top shelf, cologne smell like wood," I told him.

"Ni**a, what?" Ace yelled, then burst out laughing.

I repeated the phrase faster and waited for his response.

After a few seconds, he replied. "Okay, gotcha!" cart.

We continued talking about the family and my issue at hand: I was just sitting here. It wasn't good, but it wasn't bad. I was just ready to go.

"Aye, you should be out in a lil bit," Ace assured. "Pops said they wouldn't hold you more than 30 days."

Those words felt so anointed, I couldn't hold back my smile. "Sell that Regal, then drop off half the sack to the address I'm about to give you," I directed.

"Time's up!" a voice called from behind me.

As I made my way back to the cell, I passed Ol' School.

"I'm gone young buck!" he announced with a huge grin on his face.

"I'll see you in a few days!" I said as the officer shoved me down the hall. When I got in the cell area, I ran to the window. After a few minutes of waiting, Ol' School came out wearing a tailored suit, and I saw him get into a BMW. I didn't think he was getting to the money like that, but his lessons did speak volumes.

Two Days Later:

"Truth Toldem, today's your lucky day! You're finally being released from the facility," the bald-headed cop announced.

I had my sh*t packed and ready before he could even open the door.

"You'll be back, boy!" he taunted. But I ignored him, signing my paperwork. Through the glass door, I saw Ace sitting in the car. The thought of jumping in the passenger seat was enough to keep me silent.

"Bro, how are you up here, picking me up with no license?" I asked, getting in the car.

He brought a finger to his lips and started the car. "Everyone busy folk!" he said. He cautiously buckled his seatbelt and exited the premises.

"What you do with the bag, bro?" I asked as we cruised down the street.

"I gave it to your lawyer!" he replied. "Siegel and I put some bands with it for ya."

I sat back in the seat to digest his statement. Since the radio was turned down, so the ride got quiet.

"Bro, you gave that man all my money?" I mumbled.

He glanced at me, then looked back at the road. "We thought that was your lawyer and that you were fighting a murder case," he explained.

I wanted to get upset, but I understood his aim. I was blessed to have a solid team because that was rare in these streets.

"Bro, I f**ked up?" he asked. I looked at him for a second. I couldn't blame my brother since I didn't give him full details.

"Nah, you good!" I finally answered. "It ain't sh*t but money."

"Your girl been on the scene since you been jammed," Ace changed the subject, laughing.

"Let me use your phone, and I'll show you what's important!" was my reply. I needed to get in touch with Ol' School like yesterday since I knew my whole sack was on the line. If and when I got the sack back, I would still be in hot water with the Mexicans. Life was really throwing curve balls, but I was built for this sh*t. My team excelled in hard times.

"Hello?" he greeted.

I got so excited that he actually answered that I almost forgot the reason I called. My heart beat faster as the conversation started. I knew if everything was anointed, I could be a rich man . . . or at least a living one. I didn't know if I could trust Ol' School either because it was a dawg-eat-dawg world.

"Ol' School, it's me!" I said repeatedly until he recognized my voice. "Youngblood, what's good with ya, man?" he replied, then immediately, started talking about business. I listened closely as he gave me instructions on where to meet him.

"Youngblood, glad to hear from you. Can't wait to see you," he finished. The conversation ended as Siegel beeped in.

"Folk, folk!" he yelled into the phone.

"What's good, Siegel?" I asked. "Good to hear from ya, family!"

After my statement there was a long pause, then he said. "I'm about to beat your a** when I see you! You cost me too much money!"

I laughed and replied, "Boy, you know you wouldn't have nothing to put up if it wasn't for me! I hate when ni**as forget where they come from!"

We argued back and forth for a minute, then Siegel yelled, "Mutha-f**ker, just shoot me my one!" Then he hung up.

I was ready if he was serious because our family showed so much tough love that he might fight me for me.

"What Siegel talking about?" Ace asked, continuing down the main highway.

"Aye, where you going, bro?" I asked when I noticed he was passing Dairy Queen headed out of town.

"Bro, we gotta get you a fit so we can meet Siegel at Cafe Risque tonight," he explained. "Greenville or Anderson?"

I sat back and buckled my seatbelt. I really didn't feel like going. I'd been in jail for weeks and just wanted to take a bath and lie in my bed. However, I couldn't do anything, but ignore the fact that I couldn't go home and the fact that Ace didn't have a license. Right or wrong, I rode with him because I was loyal.

Cafe' Risque was a strip club in Lavonia, Ga. In the local newspaper, it was introduced as a new restaurant comparable to a Golden Corral or Denny's. I knew the business would be profitable because it was located right off exit on I-85. Traffic was always heavy from travelers coming to and from Atlanta. Everyone from business owners to celebrities, truck drivers, and dope boys drove on I-85N.

At first, we thought it was just a restaurant until I was on a mission to Toccoa, Ga, one night. I was coming through Lavonia and saw a nice-sized building surrounded in purple lights. It was too late for anything else to be open other than gas stations. Boom! My pull up game in full effect!

As we rode, Ace and I talked about how our lives were getting so stressful. He brought me up to speed on how hot the streets were, how much of what product we had, and how many days he projected before our well ran dry. I downloaded the information quietly, amazed at how hard we had pushed Ace and how he was well handling business.

I now understood why his mind wasn't in the books at school: Ace was born a millionaire. I remember him getting sent to the office for telling his teachers that they didn't have a big enough salary to act so boujee. No one could really say anything, though, because he was right. It just didn't seem fair to them that their truth came from a 14-year-old student.

When we arrived at the mall, Ace threw a knot of cash to me. "Aye, bro, don't spend it all at once lil ni**a."

I burst out laughing, listening to my baby brother trying to G-check me like he was a big dawg. Ace was dangerous because he gained his information from everyone. He was the youngest of a legacy created by bosses, and he had a great chance at winning, except he was born in Hartwell. We had enough money to leave and start a new life, but we couldn't pay people to buy a house and cars for us every day.

We were also too young to do anything on a big scale, and we weren't going to tell our parents about the money.

We hit the mall in Greenville, grabbed clothes and then pulled up at Twin Peaks to eat, still talking about life. At first glance, we probably looked like young, horny kids who just wanted to peep at the women, but after our order of over 50 wings and fries, no one could say anything.

I drove us back to Hartwell and immediately showered, then jumped into the bed. I woke up a few hours later to Ace' loud music. Judging from his actions, Pops must've had to work an extra shift. The bright light hurt my eyes, and the bass was making my head swim. I rolled onto my back and stared at the bottom of the top bunk. I looked at the hole in the middle. I remembered the day it was created, and how bad the pain was.

I was 12 or 13, and my parents were having yet another argument, and Pops' voice escalated. I could hear him on the other side of the door, yelling and screaming. Then, I heard bumping against the thin walls of our home. I knocked on their bedroom door, yelling for them to stop. And I wanted to make sure Mom was okay, too.

The door flew open, then Pops shouted, "Boy, you better get away from this door!"

I stood there trying to look behind and search the room. Mom was sitting on the bed, crying; but she wasn't bruised or hurt.

"Boy, get your a** out my face before I do something to you!" he yelled.

I walked back down the hallway and slammed my door. I jumped into bed and replayed the situation over and over. The thoughts of Mom being hurt heated me, so I punched the bottom bunk. I had to release the anger that I couldn't direct to Pops. I didn't understand the situation until I was old enough to date. It hit me like a ton of bricks when my girl at the time screamed at me and started to cry. Females were a lot more sensitive and emotional than men and sometimes, they cried in emotional situations. I reflected over life until I dozed off from a long day.

P.O.L.O

"Don't be on that computer all day!" Pops yelled from his room at the end of the hall.

"F**k," I whispered under my breath. Pops had bought us a computer a few years ago to keep up with the times, and Ace and I had school work that required a home computer. While the computer was great, the internet connection was dial-up.

After learning so much from Ol' School, I decided to do more research. I was impressed by his knowledge and wanted to start my own process. I knew that if one man could do it, I could, too. "You can be good at anything, as long as you practice," Pops always said. He was talking about sports when he delivered the message, but it applied to money as well.

I was missing in action for a few days as I continued learning more and more about the stock market and found it was the way of the world in many ways. For example, I could watch the stock market and pretty much figure out what would be on the news for the next few weeks. After all; gas, health care, cost of living, and industries were all we worried about.

I also studied some of the famous names in the business and researched how those individuals thought about the value of a dollar. I looked into their daily routines and how they moved money. "Make your money work for you!" was the motto they all exercised to live a lavish life.

Something else I learned was that the average American lived in debt and didn't have a clue how money worked. The lower class tried to hide their condition by spending their hard-earned money on items to impress people they didn't care for.

In my hood, this was very common. My people were hurting, and we, as strong individuals, fought the struggle with a smile. Everyone was about jokes and partying, but no one had credit. Their goals were big rims, custom gold chains, and fancy clothes, items that lost value after purchasing.

I had a few friends whose parents were middle class. Those in that bracket acted sophisticated, but carried large egos. They generally had great credit but maxed out all their credit cards just to stay afloat.

To the lower class, these individuals appeared rich, but on paper, they were dependents as well. The middle class spent money on items that held value but were liabilities and that required maintenance, like motorcycles, boats, cars, pools, vacation timeshares, etc.

The upper class consisted of the enlightened group of people. They were surrounded by sophistication and, they were unorthodox. They didn't value the opinions of others: these individuals said what and acted how they wanted because they didn't fear losing money over opinions. The majority of the high class were business owners, so never had the fear of getting fired.

I also discovered that while the upper class made a huge income, the majority were more humble than the lower classes. Many had older homes, drove non-luxury cars, and spent most of their money on assets that would pay the owner monthly to hold it.

Next Day:

"Boy, you think you slick don't ya?" Ol' School yelled, running out of the house to the car. I'd never seen him so happy: his expression let me know that the money was there and correct.

"What the f**k wrong with cuz?" Siegel asked, and Ace chuckled.

"Ya'll, chill out, and keep your eyes open for the money play," I told them as we stepped out the car.

Ol' School hugged me and slapped my back repeatedly. "You and your boys come on in the house and let's talk," he said, escorting us into the house.

When we got inside, we saw a gentleman sitting in a recliner with his legs crossed. He wore burgundy silk pajamas and leather slippers, the only time I had seen someone dress like this was the rich ones on television. He greeted each of us with a slow head nod. Then, he shuffled through a handful of papers, scanning each one through the small reading glasses balanced on the tip of his nose. They looked like bank statements from where I was.

"Truth, where the hell did you get all that money?" Ol' School asked. "You a smart lil mutha-f**ker."

I looked at Ace and Siegel for confirmation before replying. "Old School, I just came to get my cash, and be out," I told him, scanning the room for a bag. "I got some sh*t going on that's real."

I heard shuffling behind me and turned to see Ace grabbing a piece of paper from Mr. Silk Pjs. He started scanning it closely. He must have seen something interesting because he mouthed, "Damn!"

Suddenly, Ol' School clapped his hands loudly, surprising everyone. "Let's get down to business!" he suggested, then escorted us to a huge round table. When we had seated, he rubbed his hands together and observed us with a huge smile on his face.

"Thanks, Mr. Williams," he said as his sidekick placed a briefcase on the table.

Ol' School opened it, then spun it on the table in our direction. I could smell the money before the content was even exposed. The buckle of the briefcase reflected a bright light around the neatly stacked one-hundred dollar bills. The money so crisp and clean, it looked like it'd been printed right before we arrived. "Bruh, you trying to flex on us or what old man?" Siegel asked, his eyes wide at the sight of the cash.

Ol' School laughed, and Ace tapped me on the shoulder, then slid over the paper they'd been reading.

It was covered in charts and graphs and listed stock tickers and various percentage rates. I scanned the bottom of the page and read the amount $1.8 million.

"Those are some pretty big **NUM63R5**," Mr. Williams pointed out, sitting in the chair next to me. "Y'all, boys, can have all that in six months."

As I looked over the paper, the smell of cash and Mr. William's cologne filled my nose. "Was this the smell of success or a scam?" I asked myself.

"Mr. Williams has been like a brother to me," Ol' School told me. "He's been my financial coach for years. Because I trust him, he's turned into family."

I glanced at Siegel and had to hold in my laughter. He was mouthing something, so I had to read his lips. After watching him for several seconds, I read, "Ni**a, fuck that! Fuck this! Fuck this!"

I understood how Siegel felt because we'd never seen this much cash. With this much money, I could take Miguel his cash and still bring back a snow storm. I looked at Ace who was paying attention to Ol' School and Mr. William's conversation but was nodding and agreeing with getting the money. Even at the business table, Ace was hands-on like a boss.

"$800,000 of this money is yours, lil' daddy," Mr. William's said sternly, turning to me and looking in my eyes. He spread his hand wide over the money and began to slap it after each word. "I don't know what you did to invest this money, but I'm proud of ya." We wrapped up things and left.

"I gotta go hit this lick!" I yelled as I remembered Miguel. I had to come to terms with the fact that I couldn't claim this cash until somebody was dead.

I gotta do what needs to be done. The Mexican Mafia was the truth, and I knew what came behind my choices. My muscle memory kicked in; automatically, my fingers curved into position as if I was holding a pistol. I made this bed, so I had to sleep in it.

"Fuck!" I yelled as I punched the steering wheel. The horn blew, alarming Ace and Siegel. Ace turned the radio down and looked at me crazy.

"Bruh, what's wrong with you?" he asked. My heart dropped as my mind flashbacked to Dro's house. I never told the guys that the money wasn't a bonus for drug dealing. This was really some hit man sh*t about to go down. I gripped the steering wheel and pushed the gas harder.

Ace looked between me and the road repeatedly.

"I gotta tell y'all boys something," I muttered then swallowed to clear my throat. "I got to pop a mutha-f**ker, and if y'all boys don't wanna get involved I □…"

Siegel cut me off, hitting me in the chest with a fist full of cash from the backseat.

"We already know what you're about to say!" Siegel yelled. "We saw the envelope and handled that. We rich ni**a!"

He opened his hand, and the money fell covering my lap and steering wheel.

I smiled like I was overjoyed to be covered in cash, but it was just a front. Deep down, I felt like I was sinking into the seat; it was like the money weighed a ton. Yeah, I was relieved but also crushed by the words. I knew my actions were getting crazier as the money began to increase. Just like the dial increased on the speedometer of that motorcycle, we were feeling the pressure.

When we pulled into the yard, I didn't see my car, so I immediately hopped into Pops' truck and took off, back up the road. As I accelerated over the hill, I heard a faint yell. I looked in the rearview and saw Pops waving from the porch. I hesitated for a second, then continued down the road. "This will only take a second," I told myself.

I returned to my gravesite and took the shovel off the bed of the truck. Quickly, I scanned the area then began digging. I uncovered the bag stowed away with items and money; I was slick running a check up on those niggas. I felt along the seams inside the bag, then came across a small sack of cocaine that I'd put in there for I don't know what reason. When my phone rang, I threw the shovel down and grabbed it.

"Tay. . . Tay, this Truth, family!" I answered.

"I got a ball for the low. Tell me where to bring it to ya!" I explained to him.

"Bet!" I replied.

After I threw the contents back in the hole, I sped down the road toward Cross Town. I knew I had to hurry and get Pops' truck back because he looked like he was ready to have a father-son talk. I got close to town and started being trailed by a city police officer. I knew I didn't stop at the unneeded stop sign near the railroad tracks, but I didn't see the officer.

I kept my eyes on the road and the wheel steady as I maneuvered the bag out of my pocket.

"Think, Truth; think, Truth!" I said to myself.

Next thing I knew, I heard sirens and saw blue lights behind me.

I glanced down and saw the sunlight peeking through the cracks of the cover hole in the dark floorboard. I kicked the covering off and dropped the sack in the hole as I pulled the truck on the side of the road. I continued to roll slowly until the police car was parked over the bag.

My heart was about to burst out of my chest as I tried to remain calm.

He approached the car and stared at me for a few seconds.

"Son, you know why I pulled you over?" the officer questioned.

"Yes, sir! I was in a rush to take my dad's truck back," I answered.

He glanced at the side of the truck and the stickers on the window.

"You're Mr. Toldem's son?" the officer asked.

"Yes, sir, I'm on the way to take his truck back now," I answered.

He tapped the roof of the car.

"Take this truck back, but you better slow it down," he said as he walked away.

I prayed that the wind didn't blow to make the bag wave as he walked back to the cop car. I barely got out of that . . .

thanks to Pops' glory hole in the floorboard and that D.A.R.E donator's sticker on the window.

I returned the car and met Pops.

I could tell by the way he was standing - he was pissed. I slowly exited the vehicle with my head down. I didn't even want to give him eye contact, so I just began the conversation.

"You want to box or wrestle?" he yelled from the porch as I approached the stairs. "Pops chill out," I muttered again, and I cautiously attempted to pass and enter the house. I was shaking his head as if I was walking death row. Before I could turn to look at Pops, he shoved me into the wall of the house. I took the push nonchalantly and was hit in the stomach by a stiff jab. I curled around the punch and sled down the wall. "I'm tired of the constant disrespect you show me!" he yelled as he hovered over me. "If you are a man, show me you are a man and get the f**k out my spot." I stood up and began to walk down the road while I called the guys for a ride.

That night in that hotel room was the worst place, mentally, I had ever faced in life. The plush pillow followed my every move. I looked down at my feet covered with two warm blankets covered in cash. The weight of the cash was comforting as if a dog was lying in its place honoring the name of "Man's Best Friend."

The news played on TV while I listened to breaking stories, I thought about losing my family in the midst of all this crime. My lifestyle was bringing more pain than pleasure. I knew the streets didn't care about me, but the adrenaline rush I got was addictive. The high from selling to get caught and the speedometers of the things you can buy all came back to P.O.L.O. (Players Only Live Once).

I started this to get funds for my family; now I'm getting in too deep to be around them. The sick feeling started to take over my stomach as I considered whether these events were worth the cash.

"Money ain't sh*t, if you ain't doing nothing with it."

My grandfather's words echoed in my ear as I reached for the hotel phone.

"Old School, I need to talk to you, man."

The next day, Old School came to pick me up from the hotel and started training me. I stayed tucked under his wing for a few months while I stayed away from the hood. The only people who knew my whereabouts were Ace and Siegel.

I constantly reminded Old School that I wanted to give back to the hood because I felt that I helped tear it down. I knew what I wanted to do, but I couldn't even get a rental car. I needed Old School to show me the hidden figures to success.

"I'm going to turn you into a business." Old School would always say.

And he really did . . .

1. LLC - Birth Certificate
2. EIN - Social Security Number
3. Trade lines - Credit
4. Branding - Popularity

Within three months; I was back on the block. I built up enough business credit to do whatever I wanted to do - just on a bigger scale. It was the same lifestyle, but Old School transformed my entire way of thinking. I was done with the drugs and bullish*t - I was on a new journey.

I bought a small house in the country near Hartwell Lake and a few cars. I was still living life, but the police had no idea where I was because the regal was still impounded. Only thing I missed out of the whip was my CDs. I had an entire collection of nothing but black marker written labels of the best album in history.

Now, if the cops ran my car tags, it showed up Born Millionaires, LLC, as the owner. Police rarely pulled over company cars because of the status quote and the legal threat of being sued for some odd reason during the altercation. I took advantage of every moment of the kindness.

My credit cards had limits of $150k and up. Limits a social security number couldn't reach due to limited cash flow. I always got the best service and accommodations for every outlet. I gave Ace and Siegel the game and continued to increase our abilities. We started to link our business accounts together using Authorized Users, so when the EIN numbers and/or social security numbers were run through finance systems, the balances eventually became unlimited because 3 A+ rated businesses were backing one movement.

Six Months:

We had a few small businesses going in the city like car wash, lawn services, and nonprofits for the elderly and kids. Born Millionaires were starting to become a common clique in the city. We were just giving back to everyone who f**ked with us. We basically invested everything we made into another business.

One night, we were in Lavonia, Ga at Cafe' Risque, and of the women crowded around the new kings they had been hearing about. We bought rounds of drinks, going crazy for the people in the building. It was our job to make sure they knew who the f**k a Born Millionaire was.

"Truth, what's good, boy?" Siegel yelled as he split between the strippers to sit next to me.

"Bruh, I'm enjoying myself tonight - we work hard, we play hard!"

"I'm glad you said that because we just bought this bih," he yelled as he slapped my hand.

He stood up from the chair and started to yell.

"Shout out to my partner, Man Truth, because you left and came back and showed love like a real ni**a. We are the new owners of the muthaf**ker!" he shouted as the crowd roared and spilled drinks everywhere.

Next Month:

"Hello! Hello! What's up Pops . . . yeah . . . I'm doing OK . . . what time . . . I love you too."

I rolled to the end of the bed and sat up for a while. I stared at the number still displayed on the screen as I wiped my eyes. I hadn't talked to Pops since we got into that last argument. I had every intention to get over there sometime and ask forgiveness, but I didn't expect him to call first.

I put on my robe and slipper and walked to the office. I flopped into my chair as I noticed new mail, lying on my desk, that wasn't there the day before.

One looked very official, and the other envelope was handwritten. I grabbed the more official one and began to tear into the envelope. I unfolded the letter and scanned the headline.

"Welcome to the Millionaires Club!"

It was a letter telling me that my businesses had been analyzed, and everything we were doing was a tax credit. I skipped a few lines and continued to scan to get to the point faster. It seemed that I was going to receive all my start-up money back to invest back into the businesses. Those NUM63R5 gave me my second million.

I opened the next letter and scanned the page:

"I know you killed my father, and I'm going to kill you!"

"Bruh, what the f**k is this??"

www.ingramcontent.com/pod-product-compliance
Lightning Source LLC
Chambersburg PA
CBHW020435220526
45464CB00002B/716